The Stoic Cop: Policing Through Stoic Virtue

By
Bill Mauro

© 2020 by Bill Mauro. All rights reserved.

Words Matter Publishing
P.O. Box 531
Salem, Il 62881
www.wordsmatterpublishing.com

No part of this publication may be reproduced, stored in a retrieval system, or transmitted in any way by any means—electronic, mechanical, photocopy, recording, or otherwise—without the prior permission of the copyright holder, except as provided by USA copyright law.

ISBN: 978-1-949809-91-6

Library of Congress Catalog Card Number: 2020946551

Contents

Preface 1

Introduction 13

PART I: HUMILITY 21
    Us v. Them 29
    On Shit Talking 37
    On De-escalation 47
    The Letter of the Law v. The Spirit of the Law 53
    On Being Present 61
    On "Thanking Me for My Service" 65
    On Reputation 69
    On Remembering Where You Started 73
    Afterthoughts 79

PART II: VIGILANCE 85
    Training 93
    Mental Vigilance 99
    Physical Vigilance 107
    Emotional Vigilance 123
    Afterthoughts 131

PART III: TRANQUILITY 133

On Dealing with Facebook Lawyers 137
On Navigating Department Politics 143
On Surviving Police High School 147
On Being Continually Pissed Off 151
On Death 161
Hell Ain't a Bad Place to Be 169
On Reflection 177
Afterthoughts 181

PART IV: DISCIPLINE 183

The Easy Path v. The Hard Path 187
On Staying Strict 191
Grab Your Battle Ax and Start Swinging 193
Afterthoughts 197
Final Thoughts 199
Bibliography 205

THE STOIC COP: POLICING THROUGH STOIC VIRTUE

*"If wisdom were offered to me on the condition that
I should keep it shut away and not
divulge it to anyone, I should reject it."*

-Seneca-
Letters from a Stoic VI

Preface

> *"...from Rusticus I received the impression that my character required improvement and discipline."*
>
> -Marcus Aurelius-
> *Meditations 1.7*

It was late December of 2018, and I was on patrol working a 12-hour, six-month stretch of the midnight shift at my new agency. I had already been a cop for five years at this point at a different agency, and although I had worked midnights there, it was rotating shift work, meaning I switched back and forth between midnights and days monthly. Even though it was taxing on the body, I didn't mind it because the misery of the midnight shift was only eight hours long, and at four-week stretches, followed by four weeks of the normalcy of days: uninterrupted sleep, adequate sunlight, social interactions, etc.

But at my new agency, shift lengths were six months long, and for midnights that meant six months of misery. My current shift started late July, so by December, I was closing in on the end of that six months. I had a plan at the beginning of the shift that I thought would help me get through it with minimal sleep deprivation, which was to try and keep a continual midnight schedule: sleep until about 3 p.m., wake up, work out, and be at work by 7 p.m. Then get off of 7 a.m. the next day, try to be asleep by 8 a.m., and then repeat the process.

Even on my weekends, I would try to keep the exact same schedule, including staying up all night until about 5 or 6 a.m. This proved to be somewhat a good a plan at first, but the only thing that absolutely sucked was that by 7 a.m. every morning, the sun was fully up and trying to go to sleep while the sun is up on your drive home doesn't help at all, even with blackout curtains. It's the knowledge in the back of your head that the sun is fully out and life is moving on without you that really screws shit up. But besides that, the rest of my plan seemed to do me justice, that is until the winter season came along with the clock being set forward and the night setting in sooner.

Along with the days being shorter and the evenings being darker, my life too seemed to be getting darker. With the schedule I kept in the winter, I would go to be asleep by 8 a.m., wake up at around 3, sometimes even 4 p.m., and the sun would be in full setting mode by 5. I would then go to work by 7. If you do the math, during the winter months, my life literally had no more than two hours of sunlight in it if I was lucky, which is not natural. Much of my time awake was nothing but darkness, to include the weekends. Staying up all night to maintain my sleep schedule while my wife slept was the worst idea because guess what, I was sitting in darkness, watching mindless television for hours on end, and worst of all, I was alone. At least at work, I could interact with co-workers to make the night go faster and have some sort of social interaction. Needless to say, my mental health started to plummet into ways I never thought I'd allow it to go.

In the police academy, we were forced to read a book called *Emotional Survival for Law Enforcement: A Guide for Officers and their Families* by Kevin Gilmartin. For those police officers who haven't read it or even heard about it, it is definitely a good book that gives insight to the "emotional rollercoaster" we police officers go through, and how it affects our mental and emotional health. Our instructors made us read it as an independent study, in hopes to open our naïve eyes to the fact that the stress is real, the emotions are real, the job is real, and most importantly, the darkness can be real…if you let it.

But after reading it I thought that would never be me. Like any other person coming into law enforcement, I came thinking that I had already endured many obstacles in my life that I had been successful in overcoming. There was no way I would encounter something I couldn't handle.

I always had the impression that depression and suicidal thoughts were something someone could control and snap out of it at any time, but instead, people chose to be sad; and that the ones who were successful in their suicides were weak and selfish. And five years later, after a few near-death experiences, witnessing grotesque car accidents with mangled body parts, deceased bodies in pools containing a mixture of fecal matter and blood, brain dead babies from their mother exposing them to cocaine, and suicide victims with holes the size of my fist in their heads giving a clear view inside the brain cavity, I still had my emotions and mental health in check; none of that had bothered me. I figured, if I made it this far, 25 percent of my career without any psychological scarring, that I would be fine, that nothing could penetrate my inner fortress. Or so I thought until that specific December in 2018.

It was around the beginning of that month that I started to feel off, imbalanced emotionally. No motivation, no energy, no real feelings, a lot of alcohol, and highly irritable. I've gone through "moody" times in my life (I'm sure my wife and family could tell you all about that) sure, who hasn't? But this felt different. Even at my moodiest, I always had the motivation and energy to stay active, but not this time.

As the month went on, the loneliness, depression, the long weekend nights in front of the television drinking whiskey began to set in deeper, and deeper. It wasn't long after that that I began to feel worse and think worse. I'll admit it here right now for every reader something I've only admitted to two people in my life until now, I thought about killing myself because the darkness and loneliness began to actually feel unbearable.

I felt a weakness that I never once felt before in my life, and didn't know how to handle it despite there being friends, co-workers, programs and groups out there in the world that I knew I could have reached out to, but because I was at a new agency in a new state, and did not know many people in that manner that I could talk to, needless to say, it compounded the loneliness. It's funny to think now that all it took to break me down was no sunlight and lack of social interaction. It's too simple a combination. Perhaps all the stress and gore that I had witnessed over the few years had gotten to me after all; stuffed way deep down inside to where I didn't recognize it as being an issue. And now my loneliness was just the catalyst to my emotional demise.

Now, to get back on track with the story. It had been pissing down rain all night since I had gotten on shift, dragging my mood down even more. I had no motivation to deal with anyone's problems, let alone my own at that point. Sometime at around 11:50 p.m., give or take a minute or two, I got a message on my computer from a dispatcher that I needed to respond to an address in my area to do a welfare check on a detective whose GPS had shown him there for a decent amount of time. Dispatch wanted me to go out there to either make sure he was still there and okay, or if he was gone and forgot to log himself off.

After I received that message, I looked at the address on the map, but there was no detective unit showing up on the

GPS map. I thought it was weird because the map I was looking at was the same map dispatch was looking at as well. I double-checked with the dispatch to make sure she was looking at the map correctly, but she affirmed that she had a detective unit showing on the GPS at that location. I restarted my computer in hopes that the GPS on my map would reboot everyone's correct locations, but still, I did not see any detective unit out at the address dispatch wanted me to go check. Regardless though, I went and checked just in case something bad did happen to a fellow officer.

It didn't take me more than five minutes to respond to the address, in the pouring rain, to find that I had been right and there was no detective at the address dispatch gave me. Slightly annoyed, I just decided to park my cruiser in front of the house I was supposed to be checking and sit there for a few minutes to show I had made an effort.

While sitting there, the rain began to come down harder and harder, making the level of ambient noise inside my cruiser loud. I just sat, staring off into the distance contemplating why I even became a cop, and why I chose a career that brought me so much stress and aggravation at times. That's when I looked down at the clock on my laptop and saw that it was exactly midnight.

What happened next was something I can't explain. Now, if you are reading this and are expecting the world's greatest shoot out to pop off, I'm sorry to disappoint, that didn't happen here. As I looked back up from my computer through my fogged-up windshield, I could slightly see off in the distance about a block down in the middle of the dark road, a silhouette of a person walking in my direction. My first thought was to be on guard and make a plan to engage someone if they turned out to be unfriendly. My second thought was that someone needed help, but the slow, peaceful manner the figure seemed to be walking towards me, put me in a state of slight confusion. Who would be walking outside, at midnight, in pissing down rain, in the middle of the road, and without an umbrella?

As the figure inched closer towards me, I could start to see the size and shape of the person, as well as what they were wearing. I first noticed how short and frail the person seemed to be, followed by a bright red jacket, blue jeans, and baseball cap pulled down low with their head slouched towards the ground. I continued to sit in my cruiser in confusion, staring intently at the person, forehead shriveled up, eyes squinting hard, mouthing "what the fuck?" to myself in utter confusion.

All of a sudden, a friendly hand started waving, and a smiling face began to look at me. I could now see that the person was elderly. It was an elderly woman walking in the middle of the road, in the middle of the night, in the middle of a rainstorm. Despite the friendly wave and smile I received, I hopped out of my vehicle and went to see if she was in need of help.

The Stoic Cop: Policing Through Stoic Virtue

She was right next to my cruiser door at this point. I asked her if she was alright. The answer I received back shocked me. She said, "I'm just fine, I just came to see if you were alright." Confused, I replied I was fine and explained I was just checking on another officer's whereabouts. She continued to tell me, "I saw your car parked outside and something told me that I needed to check on you."

I was at a loss of words. How weird! Here I was, at the lowest point of my life, in psychological turmoil, and this sweet old woman whom I had never met or seen before in my life came to see if I was okay? What were the odds that during a rainstorm, at exactly midnight, under some weird circumstance, that I would have an encounter like this?

I began to tell her again that I was okay, even though I wasn't. I told her that she didn't need to come outside in the rain without an umbrella just for me, to which she replied, "I don't mind, it's just rain, and I'm extremely healthy in my old age."

As the conversation went on, she told me that she is an active member of her Christian parish and that she felt the Lord was looking out for me that night. She then asked if she could pray for me. Of course, I obliged. This mysterious woman then grabbed hold of my hand and prayed. After the prayer was done, she thanked me and walked back down the street to her house. I couldn't believe what had just happened. It was a sign if I had ever witnessed one. Something bigger than me had just intervened in my life, and in a good way.

Things changed for me that night. I didn't take up religion or start going to church, even though I was raised Catholic and the thought of going back to church crossed my mind. But rather, I decided I needed to make some sort of change in my life.

A few years earlier, I had purchased a copy of *Meditations* by Roman Emperor Marcus Aurelius because I had seen some quotes from it online, and they seemed like some wisdom I agreed with and could apply to my life, but I never got around to actually reading it, that is until after my revelation with this woman from the rain.

It was something about that encounter, with all its cryptic signs laid out for me, that made me pick up the book and absorb what The Roman Emperor had to say almost two thousand years earlier. I mean, the book is entitled *Meditations*, there had to be something meditative about it.

Meditations is a book of entries from the emperor's personal journals near the end of his life, written in a way that he was essentially having a conversation with himself. I picked up *Meditations* and read it slowly, one entry at a time. Slowly because the version I had was written in an almost Shakespearean style and I had to read it slowly to grasp it, but also because I really wanted to absorb and digest what Marcus was contemplating.

In the first book in the collection, Marcus details all the important people throughout his life who had instilled the wisdom that helped mold him into the virtuous leader he became, reflecting what they did to teach him and how it had helped him live contently.

As I began to read the first book, one quote stood out to me that made so much sense as to what that moment in the rain meant. The shorthanded quote reads:

> *"From Rusticus, I received the impression that my character needed improvement and discipline."*

It was at that moment that I realized the woman in the rain was my Rusticus.

As I completed the entirety of the book, I knew that there was something brilliant about this philosophy known as stoicism. I mean after all, it saved my life in some respect. I then began to study the philosophy more thoroughly, reading other works by other stoics, both ancient and modern. It wasn't long before I realized that more police officers needed to study this way of thinking and this way of life.

If one can all adopt the foundations of stoicism, then a lot of the external stressors we face can be endured by just approaching situations with a new way of thinking. I firmly began to realize that a lot of the stress we deal with is brought on by ourselves.

We don't have to allow the fact that there are people out there who are anti-police bother us, or we don't have to get bummed out over rudeness complaints if we had just maintained a cool head to begin with, or we don't have to worry about getting caught in a lie if we had just been truthful with everyone, especially ourselves. We don't have to allow any of those scenarios, or the unlimited number of other scenarios torture us if we just keep in mind that although we can't control what happens in life, we can control our decisions and our reactions to external situations.

If we strive to live a virtuous life, then a lot of those big problems we find ourselves in only become smaller and easier to accept. It all begins with recognizing that your character requires improvement and discipline.

Introduction

What is stoicism? Stoicism is a philosophy founded around 300 B.C. by Zeno of Citium. The teachings stressed the importance of being able to find inner peace (eudaimonia) in the midst of the chaotic external world around us; being able to recognize what is in our control (our perception and will) and what is not in our control (death, material objects, other people, etc.), and how to remain detached (apatheia) from those things not in our control. And when I say chaos, I mean the chaos that is relative to us, our own perceived chaos we encounter daily masked as stress.

For example, as humans, we all tend to be creatures of habit, so when something abruptly changes in our schedule, some may tend to view it as chaotic and stressful. In law enforcement, stress can be as simple and unimportant as not being able to get your morning cup of coffee before hitting the streets because calls for service start pouring in as soon as you get to work, to being in a full-fledged, unexpected volley of gunfire with an individual who took you by surprise, and then everything else that falls in between. Although at opposite ends of the stress spectrum, those two examples do plague us and, if we allow it, can dictate how the rest of our day goes.

But take a second to examine those examples. Is either of those circumstances completely within our control? Can we control if a ton of calls for service interrupts our morning coffee ritual, or if some coward decided they wanted to unexpectedly take a shot at us? Of course not, so we must control how we respond to it. We must not allow it to freeze us up and cannot allow it to affect us in the long run.

Of course, being shot at is highly stressful and chaotic, and every instinct you have may cause you to be shaken up at the moment, but you can learn to not lose your nerve. You can be effective in that situation with sound decision making, if you learn to understand the importance of getting your mindset right beforehand, realizing that you cannot control what just happened, and only control how you react to it.

Are you going to have a warrior mindset and end the situation? Are you going to learn from it and take away a great deal of experience and understanding from it? Or are you going to cower and quit?

That is what stoicism teaches, how to deal with the chaos graciously, with benevolence, a clear head and with acceptance. Being able to acquiesce and see the silver lining in the bad, and gifts they can bring forth, make good decisions amid the chaos, and ultimately to live contently despite it all.

Epictetus, born into slavery around 55 A.D. is regarded as one of the most influential of the ancient Stoics. He believed and was recorded as saying in the book *Discourses*:

"It is we who torment, who make difficulties for ourselves; that is, our opinions do."

He also said in the *Enchiridion*:

"It is not the events that disturb people, it is their judgments concerning them."

On September 9, 1965, Vice Admiral James Bond Stockdale had his plane shot out of the sky over Vietnam, causing him to eject from the cockpit and descend into enemy territories. He described having only thirty seconds before he landed to get his mind right. As a student of stoicism himself, and a follower of Epictetus' teachings from the *Enchiridion*, he said to himself during the descent knowing well that he was about to be captured and enslaved by the enemy, "Five years down there, at least. I am leaving the world of technology and entering the world of Epictetus."

Over the course of the next eight years, Vice Admiral Stockdale was a prisoner of war in a Vietnamese camp, as well as being brutally beaten for four of them while also held in solitary confinement. He then detailed in his essay, *Courage Under Fire: Testing Epictetus' Doctrines in a Laboratory of Human Behavior*, how he applied the stoic philosophy to guide him through those horrible eight years, realizing that he could not control the situation, only controlling his reasoned choice and reactions.

And because he kept his mind an impenetrable fortress, he never once gave the Vietnamese any information they wanted. He also survived his P.O.W. years, going on to retire with thirty-seven years with the United States Navy. He was the only three-star officer in the history of the Navy to wear both aviator wings and the Congressional Medal of Honor. Vice-Admiral Stockdale also held twenty-six combat decorations during that time as well.

He was a supreme example of what stoicism is all about the ability to have the discipline inside your mind to endure all obstacles, no matter how painful they may be, and persevering; coming out the other side on top.

But on the greener side of things, simply put, what stoicism aims to achieve is how to live happily through virtue and in accordance with what nature has prescribed and laid out for us. I'm sure that sounds vague so to break it down farther, ancient stoics focused on four cardinal virtues: wisdom, courage, temperance, and justice.

- Wisdom is knowing/recognizing how to feel and act accordingly towards the external, physical world.
- Courage is knowing/recognizing how to feel and act accordingly when the external, physical world opposes or challenges you.

- Temperance is knowing the balance of emotion needed in order to feel and act correctly towards the external, physical world.
- Justice is knowing how to feel and act correctly towards others in the external, physical world.

The ancient Stoics believed that a concentration in these virtues was in accordance with nature, and the avenue to achieve inner peace.

All four virtues are dependent on each other. For example, a mastery in temperance will help moderate just how courageous you should be in each situation. Too much courage can lead to overconfidence and reckless decision making. While not enough courage will result in a failure to act in the heat of battle. Another example being, if you don't hold the wisdom to recognize the correct application of the law, how can you issue justice correctly?

Since discovering Marcus Aurelius' *Meditations* during my darkest hour, and furthering my understanding of the stoic philosophy, I began to realize that a lot of what the Stoics taught on how to be virtuous is severely lacking in law enforcement today. And with this lack of virtue, the disconnected gap between police and citizens widens, integrity diminishes, characters become flawed, stress turns into a fatal demon, and the fraternal *thin blue line* begins to blur at times.

While the ancients believed that wisdom, courage, temperance, and justice were the big four, I've come to realize through my experience as a police officer and countless hours of study, that we should also place value on humility, vigilance, tranquility, and discipline. Those are our big four, cardinal virtues which I aim to break down and explain with this book because I believe them to correlate befittingly to what a virtuous police officer is.

My intent when I started this project is not to preach or criticize or sell you on some empty religion; but just to start a conversation about how altering your perspective on stress and chaos can help subdue your inner anguish. I am aware that stoicism has taken on a great resurgence into popular culture over the past few years, and a lot of the ideas and connections I make have been said and connected before by others, I realize that. But my goal is to help bridge the gap between stoicism and law enforcement because, well, I don't believe that anyone else has done that yet.

With the aid of stoic aphorisms, I have humbled myself down to a state of vulnerability to retell stories of times where I wasn't a good person or a good cop. I have connected the dots between the philosophy and the profession as it pertains to my life, and hopefully, this will help you, the police officer or curious citizen, make your own connections.

I want police officers to know that through stoic philosophy, there is nothing an officer can't endure whether it be department politics, unruly criminals, or the darkness inside their personal lives. By opening this up, you have agreed to be willing to listen, think, possibly change and grow. In order to do this, you must come to understanding with yourself as best described by Epictetus:

> *"If you want to make progress, put up with being perceived as ignorant or naïve on worldly matters, don't aspire to a reputation of sagacity."*

So, as I have made myself and my stories vulnerable to you, I ask that you do the same when trying to learn from this. Humble yourself, be truthful with yourself, recognize your faults and weaknesses, and grow from them, even if people question your actions. Ultimately, learn to control your perceived chaos.

PART I

~~~~~~~~

HUMILITY

"An unhealthy belief in our own importance. Arrogance. Self-centered ambition. It's that petulant child inside every person, the one that chooses getting his or her way over anything or anyone else. The need to be better than, recognized for, far past any reasonable utility—that's ego."

-Ryan Holiday-
Ego is the Enemy

Ryan Holiday wrote an entire book on just how detrimental ego can be if we do not utilize our temperance properly. The book he wrote is literally titled; *Ego is the Enemy*. It is important to note that our egos are beneficial to us in ways. Ego is the driving force that motivates us to achieve goals, to beat adversarial odds, and prove people who don't believe in our capabilities wrong. But it is such a delicate characteristic in our psyche that if we don't recognize it and keep it in check, if we can't apply a brake to it, ego can literally drive us into a wall causing us to hurt ourselves or worse, others. And if you've read *The Wolf of Wall Street* or seen the movie, you know how extreme ego can be a ticking time bomb as depicted by the life of Jordan Belfort.

Unfortunately, having a big ego is a problem that I've seen plague the law enforcement profession. Men and women who don't like to be wrong in front of the public eye, and who can't admit when they actually are wrong. Officers who refuse to or cannot de-escalate situations, who feel they need to talk over others instead of listening in order to get to the root of the problem and solve it. Cops who are *too good* or *too knowledgeable* to accept criticism from other cops, or train regularly, or stay on top of changing case laws. And the cops who just can't be told "no" from a citizen, even if they have the right to say no in certain circumstances. I've admittedly and embarrassingly been that cop.

Every single cop who reads this has been there. You have, at times, had an oversized ego and probably didn't even realize it in the moment. Don't lie to yourself now, because stoicism is about being truthful with yourself. I remember as a rookie, back when writing traffic citations was the easiest stat to get where everyone got a ticket, even for frivolous equipment violations, without taking any other deciding factors into consideration.

Later, I found myself thinking that maybe I didn't really need to give that person a ticket, a warning probably would have sufficed because they weren't rude, and it was just an honest equipment violation that we've all been guilty of.

Despite my perceived awareness of myself as being a professional, my actions were all ego-based and that is what is so dangerous about it. Our ego tells us that we're humble, that we've got ourselves in check and that we aren't irrationally handing down frivolous justice.

Where does this oversized ego come from? My theory, through my experience and research, lies in this:

In 1971, Dr. Philip Zimbardo conducted a social experiment at Stanford University on the psychology of perceived power, called the *Stanford Prison Experiment.* The experiment was set to be two weeks in length, but only lasted six days between August 14-20 which during that time, he assigned two different roles to a group of volunteering students: one group would be prisoners stripped of most of their clothing and given smocks to wear, and the other group would be guards and given wooden batons, mirrored glasses, and uniforms. The groups of students he selected were screened for any prior experience in the criminal justice system, as well as having a healthy mental and emotional base.

During the course of the experiment, the students embraced their roles assigned to them, specifically the guards who, with their assigned power and authority, were reported to have begun to abuse their powers in almost a sadistic fashion. Obviously, it was the newfound power that inflated the egos of the roleplaying guards causing them to act in a way that they probably wouldn't have normally acted without their given powers.

I would never claim that we as police are sadistic as a whole, even though there are those few bad apples out there, but we have to be aware that when we get that gun and badge, that it really does subconsciously bolster our egos, give us this overbearing sense of power that we may have never experienced before; and if we are not careful, if we don't recognize it, then we will be unsuccessful in the service were are supposed to be providing. The last thing we want to do in public service is to be perceived as a tyrant, a sadist, an asshole, etc. I like to remember this:

> *"Appearances are deceiving. Having the authority is not the same as being an authority. Having the right and being right are not the same either."*
>
> -Ryan Holiday-

To me, this means that just because I have been afforded the right to make someone do something doesn't always mean that I have to make someone do something. Every situation is different and utilizing discretion successfully truly shows your ability as a cop to be humble. Being unable to utilize discretion at all, and policing by force in ever single scenario truly shows how blinded you are by ego.

Upon reading thus far, you'd probably have assumed by now that I've been talking strictly about citizen interactions when it comes to checking ego. And although that is the larger part of the picture, there is another part; the lesser understood, undermined, or unrealized part. Interactions with fellow officers within the profession, more importantly within your own agency.

Too many times I have come across supervisors with huge egos who have no respect from their subordinates, senior officers with huge egos who would rather talk shit and complain about rookies instead of helping them or molding them into better officers, and lastly officers with huge egos who would rather stab others in the back in hopes of having a better shot at promotions. Egos amongst each other tend to make me question at times if the *Thin Blue Line* really exists. So, what is the answer to remedy ego? Answer; practicing humility.

In 1989, the movie *Roadhouse* was released which featured Patrick Swayze as the character Dalton, a reformed philosophical bouncer, known for his ability to turn rough bars around through verbal de-escalation. This is relevant because I remember being in training during a type of de-escalation class called *verbal judo*, where the instructor played the scene from the movie where Dalton is addressing his security staff about how to conduct themselves in situations. He begins by saying:

The Stoic Cop: Policing Through Stoic Virtue

> "All you have to do is follow three simple rules. One, never underestimate your opponent. Expect the unexpected. Two, take it outside. Never start anything inside the bar unless it's absolutely necessary. And three, be nice."

Of course, the "be nice" part was met with criticism by the other characters in the movie, as well as the peers in my training class. Dalton then goes onto say:

> "If somebody gets in your face and calls you a cocksucker, I want you to be nice. Ask him to walk. Be Nice. If he won't walk, walk him. But be nice. If you can't walk him, one of the others will help you. And you'll both be nice. I want you to remember that it's just a job. It's nothing personal. I want you to be nice until it's time not to be nice."

Although a Hollywood movie, there is much sense behind that scene once you put the ideas into action. But the hard part is just that, putting it into action because we are led to believe that in order to make people do things and listen to us, we must show force, we need to "peacock," flare our chests out and be an authoritative presence. There is a huge lesson to be learned from the character Dalton in that movie, and that lesson is in humility. Humility is the exact opposite of Ryan Holiday's quote about ego at the beginning of this chapter; it is defined as a modest or low view of one's self-importance or humbleness.

Dalton exemplifies just how realistic it is to solve problems with complete humility while also being an authoritative presence. Not allowing ego to get in the way of acting rationally, taking the higher ground, and portraying a decorum worth respecting. But he also leaves the door open for the need to be forceful when the time comes when he says, "be nice until it's time not to be nice." If you're skeptical about buying into Hollywood effects, then consider Epictetus' teaching from the Enchiridion where he says:

> *"For every challenge, remember the resources you have within you to cope with it. Provoked by the sight of a handsome man or beautiful woman, you will discover within you the contrary power of self-restraint. Faced with pain, you will discover the power of endurance. If you are insulted, you discover patience. In time, you will grow to be confident that there is not a single impression that you will not have the moral means to tolerate."*

He is saying that we all have learned in our lifetime abilities on how to cope with difficult situations, problems, and people. We just have to practice using them, and that starts with deflating ego and utilizing humility. Humility will clear our muddy judgments and guide us in finding those abilities we have to endure the situation and treat others fairly and justly. Be nice until it's time not to be nice.

Us v. Them

On August 9, 2014, in a suburb of St. Louis, Missouri known as Ferguson, Officer Darren Wilson was out on patrol when he had responded back-up to a theft in progress from a local marketplace. The description of the suspect was a black male wearing a white T-shirt, St. Louis Cardinals hat, yellow socks, and khaki shorts who had fled the scene with a stolen box of Swisher cigars.

Not long after responding to the area Officer Wilson encountered a subject matching that description, later identified as Michael Brown. What happened next has been widely debated by opposing witness accounts, but what is known is that a struggle between Officer Wilson and Brown ensued, resulting in Brown being fatally shot. What was so controversial was not just the fact that Officer Wilson was white and Brown was black, but because witness accounts claimed that Brown was unarmed, retreated, and had his hands up when Officer Wilson shot him.

The Stoic Cop: Policing Through Stoic Virtue

Later, forensic evidence suggested that Brown engaged Wilson while he was sitting in his police-issued vehicle and began to attack him, prompting Officer Wilson to fear for his life and shoot Brown. Officer Wilson was then cleared of criminal charges, as well as civil rights violations. We all know what happened next.

The citizens of Ferguson, Missouri, along with citizens from 170 other cities within the United States to include St. Louis, Philadelphia, Seattle, Albuquerque, New York, Cleveland, Los Angeles, Oakland, Chicago, Minneapolis, Atlanta and Boston, primarily made up of the African-American population, erupted into violent protests; burning vehicles, looting stores, and destroying property. All in the name of perceived racial inequalities and perceived police brutality despite forensic evidence.

Prior to the Ferguson shooting, plainclothes officers with the New York Police Department (NYPD) had been accused of the negligent death of a black male, identified as Eric Garner, when they were seen on video placing Garner in what appeared to be a chokehold while Garner was stating that he could not breathe. When Garner subsequently passed away from the incident, non-violent protesting had ensued across many cities in the United States. The death of Eric Garner at the alleged hands of the NYPD was essentially fuel for the riots that followed the Ferguson incident.

And of course, post-Ferguson, there were many more nationally recognized police incidents where African-American individuals were killed during police encounters where the officer was found to be justified. Those incidents added more fuel to the fire and tightened the tension between police agencies and the African-American community across the nation. Those incidents were: The Alton Brown shooting in Baton Rouge, LA, the death of Freddie Gray in Baltimore, MD, the shooting of Philando Castile in St. Paul, MN, and the death of Sandra Bland in Waller County, TX. Ultimately these all sparked a surge of the Black Lives Matter (BLM) movement where members of the movement were extremely active and vocal against police departments across the United States.

All of a sudden, officers were getting ambushed while sitting in their vehicles, getting ambushed while arriving on scene to a call for service, getting their names dragged through the mud in the news, and having their lives and careers tarnished. And the tensions have remained relatively high since then.

Where was I in 2014 at the start of the Eric Garner and Michael Brown incident? I was currently in what is probably the most primitive, formative and influential part of a cop's career, I was in the Field Training program. And there I was learning and soaking in how police work is done, observing tactics, listening to how to utilize communication skills, practicing investigative skills, etc. But what I was also observing was the response to the national state of affairs by senior officers. And as you would guess, the mentality was that "we," as in the brotherhood of police, were under attack.

It didn't help that also at the same time, the agency and city I had been employed in had its own officer-involved shooting where an African-American suspect, who had been apprehended into handcuffs on criminal charges, had brandished a hidden firearm on his person and attempted to shoot at an officer. That officer was able to fire first and ultimately killed the suspect. But because the officer was white, the suspect being a handcuffed black man, and a city with a large African-American demographic (roughly a little higher than 80%), needless to say, there were some small protests in my city. Thankfully they were not large or violent ones, but I, a white police officer, was viewed as the enemy and I felt it with almost every encounter I had with a member of the African-American community.

So, I began to embrace the *Us. v. Them* mentality. I was skeptical of everyone's actions and intentions on every call that I rode on and rightfully so. Cops were getting ambushed across the nation and I did not want to be another casualty, so I became hyper-vigilant, suspect, and calloused towards everyone I encountered, even towards those who wanted to thank me for my service because I just didn't believe anyone to be sincere. I had really just turned into a cynical asshole towards everyone.

Realistically, this type of mentality is purely ego-driven and we tend to lack the humility to empathetically realize that maybe the groups of people who are peacefully protesting, who do feel that they have been targeted, are much different from those who violently protest, and have a constitutional right to speak their minds. Our egos won't let us see their point of view because "we are the police and how dare any groups of people disrespect us," right?

It's important to be vigilant and aware of people at times in this line of work, especially in times of political and social tension, but do we have to lack an equal understanding of opposing views simply because of our egos? Of course not.

I'm not sure when the exact moment was where I began to realize just how ridiculous the *Us v. Them* mentality was getting within the law enforcement profession, but I know that it turned us all into a bunch of whiny children.

Soon I began to realize just how overly sensitive cops were getting at the most minuscule, unimportant, or arbitrary sign of disrespect from the public. There were headlines in the news about cops being denied service at a coffee shop in their areas for whatever reason the employee had to refuse them service, and then all of a sudden, cops all over social media were condemning the entire franchise to hell instead of that particular employee, and being *triggered*.

There were plenty of these types of disrespectful stories making headlines, but one in particular that I finally just rolled my eyes at was a story in November of 2019 where a police officer walked into a local Starbucks for his coffee and gave the barista his name. When he received his cup of coffee, instead of his name being written on the cup, he noticed it said the word "pig" on it. Next thing you know, it made national news, and as I mentioned before, cops everywhere requested the termination of the barista and swore to never drink Starbucks again, as they had done and said in the past.

I can't help but roll my eyes at stories like that. Are our egos that fragile that a word such as "pig" throws us into a frenzy of social media protest? And if there was a concern over the cup of coffee being tampered with, the officer could have just thrown it out and gone somewhere else. A humble and stoic cop would have already been at peace realizing the fact that not everyone likes the police and not everyone will. He or she would have then quietly thrown the cup out, left the establishment and found their coffee elsewhere.

But instead, cops turn into the same "snowflakes" that they like to ridicule on social media. What's the remedy for the extreme side of the *Us v. Them* mentality? You guessed right, humility. Having the humility to realize that we have allowed our opinions and poorly moderated emotions turn us into triggered un-professionals. We have to recognize, as Epictetus said,

"If someone succeeds in provoking you, realize that your mind is complicit in the provocation."

The *Us v. Them* mentality isn't a new phenomenon though, it's been around decades, which may explain why the relationship between police and citizens is so deteriorated today (media depiction aside). *Us v. Them* only works when there is a clear-cut enemy. In most military wars throughout history, enemies are usually clearly defined and easily identifiable with a uniform, so the mentality works in that way.

However, in law enforcement, there is no clearly defined enemy. We deal with citizens of the United States of America, so really there is no enemy, just a percentage of the population that chooses to do bad things. It is actually un-American to pigeonhole any other American as an enemy.

And even though there are evil Americans living amongst our society who need to be dealt with, there is still an expectation that their rights are preserved, and justice and fairness are upheld. This is what makes our jobs so difficult.

Having an *Us v. Them* state of mind still does have its place though, amid violent, high stress, rapidly evolving situations. It's the type of mentality that will guide you in your perseverance in winning the fight, but that's where it should end; with the fight. No longer maintain your hyper-vigilance with everyone you meet. Not everyone is an enemy who hates the police.

Whatever the political or social climate is, you don't have to be at war with everyone, including those who are ignorant. Learn to control your reactions to situations, moderate your emotions, and change your perspective to learn why some person felt the need to be disrespectful towards you.

Once you take a step back, try having a conversation and influence their perception of you as you try to alter your perception of them. If they don't want to have a conversation, fine, that's why you're the professional and they're not. It shouldn't even bother you past that point.

ON SHIT TALKING

"The best way of avenging yourself is not to become like the wrongdoer."

-Marcus Aurelius-
Meditations 6.6

In April of 2015, I had been operating as a police officer on solo status for only 6 months. I had received an anonymous call early one morning right before I was about to get off after working all night on the midnight shift of a suspicious male walking around a neighborhood throwing rocks at the window of the house. Needless to say, I was filled with anger on my way to this call. I had worked all night, I was exhausted, and minutes away from getting called back to the precinct so I could go home.

When I received the call, I hesitated for a few seconds to see if the day shift sergeant was going to get on the radio and advised dispatch to hold the call for day shift units, but the sergeant never did, and I ultimately had to respond with pure frustration inside.

The Stoic Cop: Policing Through Stoic Virtue

In minutes, I had arrived on the scene and found the subject matching the description standing in the yard of the house which he was accused of throwing rocks at. The male was young, in his early twenties, tall and slim. When I made contact with him, I advised him of the complaint we had received and asked him what he was doing. He was calm and cooperative, but I was still slightly annoyed at this point.

He told me that he was waiting on his girlfriend to come outside and that he was throwing rocks at her window to get her attention. This made no sense. Why would an adult male have to throw rocks at his girlfriend's window to get his girlfriend's attention instead of just knocking on the door? There was something more to it. When I asked him why he wasn't waiting inside the house for his girlfriend, he stated that her aunt was not fond of him, leading me to believe that he was not welcome on the property, especially since it was 7 o'clock in the morning.

I then went up to the residence and made contact with the occupants inside hoping to clear the air of what was really going on and perhaps solve this issue civilly and without any paperwork. An older female had opened the door and let me in. It turns out that she was the one who called the police and was also the aunt of the male's girlfriend. The girlfriend was also present inside and told me that this male subject was in fact her ex-boyfriend, who had some issues, and the aunt confirmed that he was not welcome on the property and wanted him to leave.

Now I was even more frustrated. Not only had the male lied to me, which I absolutely hated at that point, but now I was obligated to make an arrest right when I was about to get off of work since it was a borderline domestic-related incident, and a loitering and prowling charge was pretty apparent.

I reinitiated contact with the male subject and began to place him under arrest. Of course, he was upset that I was arresting him. I was explaining to him the circumstances of him not being allowed on the property. He asked who it was that didn't want him on the property, the aunt or his girlfriend. I snidely replied, "Both."

I'm not sure why he chose to do what he did next. Whether it was because he knew he was going to jail or the fact that I told him that his ex-girlfriend also didn't want him on the property, or perhaps both, but it all happened in slow motion.

As I had him in what is known as an *escort position*, standing next to my classic Crown Victoria near the back window, just about ready to place him inside, I felt the male wind his head backward, and then thrash it forwards with an immense force into the back window of my patrol car; causing his face to go completely through it.

The back windows of any vehicle, for safety reasons, are tempered glass, which is four times stronger than standard glass, so needless to say, the force in which this male put his face through the window was extremely great and caused very obvious and deep lacerations.

The Stoic Cop: Policing Through Stoic Virtue

As I watched and felt his face shatter a hole in my back window, the first split-second reaction I had was pure shock and awe. In my few short months as a police officer, I had never seen or experienced a suspect do something this extreme. Of course, a struggle then ensued as the initially calm demeanor male at the beginning of the incident, had done a 180 and turned into a byproduct of the *Exorcist*. I took him to the ground as be began kicking, screaming, and flailing around, trying to control and restrain him despite the fact that he was already in handcuffs. That's when I noticed the blood exploding out of his face like a geyser with every yell he let out. I immediately called for EMS.

He yelled out all sorts of things about how I put his face through the window, about how he wanted me to kill him, and about he was going to kill his girlfriend. He made a huge scene that caused people to start gathering outside their homes in the early hours of the morning to see what was going on.

It wasn't long before he attempted to grab at my gun saying that he was going to use it to kill himself. He also began to spit his blood at me and other officers and EMT's, while saying that he had AIDS and was going to infect us with it. Two sedatives were then deployed by EMT's to try and curb his rage, but they didn't work. This individual was committed.

At that point, the anger, frustration, and annoyance I had prior to the outburst, got the best of me and I began talking shit back to this individual. I would answer every threat and name he threw at me with my own barrage of insults which would then escalate his physical resistance and verbal abuse while I and three other officers were trying to restrain him to an ambulance gurney.

He had gotten the best of me which resulted in me stooping down to his level and escalating the situation. What I was essentially doing was making our job harder. If I had just let this male play out his temper tantrum, although bloody and violent, without giving him the response he desired, the situation could have been handled more efficiently. My actions didn't go unnoticed. The sergeant on duty had been observing my behavior.

The next day, I was approached by my direct sergeant. He told me that the other sergeant had let him know how I had handled that high-stress situation. Not that I made any potentially fatal tactical errors, or hesitated in fear, or didn't get the job done, but because I aided in the escalation of that male's violent behavior. My sergeant told me that the other sergeant wanted me to be written up, but he had talked her into letting him give me a verbal counseling on how to behave in times like that.

Even though I didn't get in any serious trouble, I still took it personally. I told myself I had gotten the job done. So what if I talked a little shit to the guy? In my mind at the time, he deserved it. But that was my ego. My ego was what drove me to lower my professionalism, lower my standards, abandon my discipline, and talk shit to the guy even though I was trained to conduct myself better than people like that, and not give them the response they want.

It was also my ego that had gotten offended and upset at that sergeant who wanted to have me written up. And ultimately, it was my ego and my choice that allowed that male to get under my skin and allow myself to make excuses for my behavior. Again, referring back to Epictetus:

> "It is not the events that disturb us, it is our judgments towards them."

My judgments before the moment, in the heat of the moment, and after the moment were poor. My reactions were poor, and therefore it had disturbed my ego.

What I didn't ask myself at the time, and wouldn't realize for a few years, was what if I had figured out that I had won the fight before I even took that male into custody? He had been calm the entire time, I had placed him under arrest and into handcuffs with no fight and was about to place him the back of my vehicle to seal the deal.

But when I think about it, perhaps it was my frustrated, condescending attitude towards him during the arrest stage that may have pushed him over the edge. When he asked me about which person didn't want him at the house, his ex-girlfriend or her aunt, I didn't realize then that everything that transpired after was a result of the deliverance of that answer.

He didn't want to hear me say his ex-girlfriend didn't want him there. Hearing that more than likely shattered him. He wanted me to say that the aunt and only the aunt didn't want him. He probably would have been more understanding of that since he already knew that the aunt did not like him.

Not that I'm condoning his behavior prior to the situation since he was still committing a crime, but I could have shown more humility in my approach. Instead of answering like a frustrated, angry asshole announcing that both women didn't want him there, perhaps I could have delivered the answer more professionally or just lied and said only the aunt.

When I think about it now, it was a combination of the answer he didn't want to hear plus being delivered in a way he felt disrespected which may have catapulted him into the fit of rage that erupted afterward. I wish I could have remembered that line, "Be nice until it's time not to be nice." Perhaps the end result would have been less violent.

I can't say that I learned my lesson right there and then after that incident, but that incident, along with more experience on the street, helped me begin to realize that once the fight is over, whether it be physical or not, so should the shit-talking.

Being on calls as a backup for other officers who made arrests had put me in a more detached position, where I was able to see firsthand how unnecessary talking shit to a guy in handcuffs is. First, it pisses the arrestee off and more often than not causes them to become disorderly, which results in you having to deal with that headache. And second, it's demeaning.

Again, I'm not condoning criminal behavior, never would. I'm not saying that there aren't some people out there in the world who are evil, but what I am saying, in the majority of instances in basic police work, especially patrol, the people you arrest primarily are people who have made simple, dumb mistakes.

They know deep down they screwed up, and most likely they're embarrassed, which is why they resort to talking shit to you first, as a knee-jerk defensive reaction to their embarrassment. Say what you will about the justice system, but try and remember what the exact goal of the justice system is; the goal ultimately is to try to correct criminal behavior through various means of punishment. And guess what? The rehabilitation starts with you.

You, the police officer, are the first encounter the accused has in the justice system. What kind of motivation is the accused going to have to try and correct themselves if their first impression of the justice system is an unprofessional asshole? The answer is, not a lot of motivation, first impressions are everything.

Even though you may be a small part of the often drawn-out and arduous process of the justice system, the fact remains that you are still a part of it. And a system or process has no chance of working unless all of its parts work together towards the goal.

You know the role you've been assigned to do because you signed up for it, and you know how to do it justly because you've been trained. Deviation from that role has seldom gotten any officer in a great amount of trouble from the brass, nor has it created any grief or shame deep down inside. Act professionally at all times, be aware of what you say to people, as well as how you say it.

On De-Escalation

"The supreme art of war is being able to subdue the enemy without fighting."

-Sun Tzu-
The Art of War

Remember that you're policing in an era where de-escalation is a hot topic issue. Frequently, videos surface online depicting cops having to use force on individuals, some who are armed and some who are not, and usually the first comments posted on social media, besides the ever-popular racial or social injustice ones, are "why couldn't the cops de-escalate the situation better?"

Granted, those comments are proposed by people who don't understand policing, who don't understand the totality of circumstances, the necessary and reasonableness standards, use of force continuums, etc. Even though they do not understand the totality of what they are watching in the videos, obviously de-escalation is still a concern for them, as so it should be for us. I mean, who really likes having to fight people when successful de-escalation tactics are the better option? Especially with an armed person.

Sun Tzu had this inclination 2,500 years ago, and his writings are still circulating today amongst many successful organizations to include the upper echelons of our military, so there is obviously something to de-escalation, right? That is why de-escalation classes are starting to become a requirement in basic academy classes, as well as yearly refresher courses across many states to include crisis intervention team (CIT) training, as well as verbal judo as I mentioned previously.

There's a stigma in law enforcement amongst cops that the tactics taught in those classes don't work, and if they are selected ("voluntold") to participate in those classes, they do not take them at all seriously, and why? Because of Ego, the force field that causes the inability to learn something new. As Epictetus put it:

> *"It is impossible for a person to begin to learn what they think they already know."*

I have been guilty of that. Being too egotistical and stubborn to adapt to new ideas because I was too set in my ways. And furthermore, there is also a stigma when it comes to the mental health community. We as police get called to residences all the time where mental health patients, usually not very lucid, are having episodes of paranoia or hallucinations, and they are also usually the same citizens who call in on a frequent basis. And our initial reaction is to get frustrated before we even get there because we already perceive their complaints to be bullshit. And when we get on scene, our frustration is perceived by the mental patient negatively, which then causes them to escalate their behaviors which can make it harder to quell the situation and/or result in avoidable confrontations. I have also been guilty of that as well.

It wasn't until I implemented some humility on a particular call where I realized just how well de-escalation techniques work in resolving these types of situations while preserving the dignity of the patient and showing them respect. They are people too after all.

But before I get into that call, let me brief you on the background of the individual I will talk about. During my tenure at my first agency, I worked a particular beat that had a lot of mental patients residing in it. There was this one woman in particular who was a highly paranoid schizophrenic patient, but who was deemed by medical professionals to be able to live on her own, although still monitored by a program to make sure she was taking her medications and taking care of herself. Although medicated, she still heard voices.

As an almost nightly occurrence, she would call the police to report people having sex in her attic, as well as people spying on her. And of course, as a nightly occurrence, I would roll my eyes and wonder why our call center wouldn't screen just this call because, after all, we all knew her name, address, and reputation by heart very well.

Then I would arrive on the scene and be disgruntled, as well as disgusted because her entire house smelled like urine (she wore adult diapers) which was augmented because she kept the heat on in her house very high all year long. She would then explain to me her fictitious complaint (although to her it was very real) and then I would arrogantly dismiss it and be on my way, failing to give her mind any solace in regards to what she was experiencing.

Then on one particular afternoon, when I was working day shift, I received a call to the local hospital in regards to an emotionally distraught person near the employee picnic tables. As I got on the scene, I could see that it was the same woman who I had dealt with many times before on the night shift. And she was definitely having an emotional episode, crying, screaming, almost like a toddler during a temper tantrum.

I also noticed another officer who had been working off-duty at the hospital, as well as one of the security guards employed by the hospital trying to calm her down. The off-duty officer was trying to get her attention but was not having any luck; I also noticed his hand on his Taser, not because she was actively assaulting anyone or actively armed, but just ready to use it if at any time the situation went to hell in a handbag quickly.

Emotionally distraught people can be very unpredictable. I recognized that if we couldn't de-escalate the situation verbally, then it could escalate to something worse. I knew I had to step in and utilize humility.

Having a prior knowledge of this individual was a huge step in the de-escalation process. According to Force Science Institute (FSI), there are five steps to process:

1. The first step is having a good understanding and background information of the situation, which I already seemed to have.
2. The second step is making contact with the person, actual contact, meaning having their attention, and because I was familiar with her, I knew her name so I called it out to her. This got her attention which was a big step in order to begin a conversation with her.
3. The third step is staying calm. Talking gently with a sense of empathy goes a long way. Once you allow your emotions to escalate personally, that could cause the distraught person to escalate as well. So, I began to talk to this woman as soothingly as I could, asking her if she recognized me so that she was able to connect to some sort of familiar face.
4. The fourth step is focusing on the goal which is to de-escalate and get to the root of the problem. By getting her attention and being able to control the energy

of the conversation, I was able to get her to tell me why she was upset. And it was simple, she had simply gotten lost walking home from the doctor's office and panicked, completely understandable for person suffering from a mental illness. By now understanding her problem, I was now able to offer solutions of her choosing. Because it stems into the fifth step

5. The fifth step is realizing that although you can, as the cop, try and control the flow of the conversation, you can't control the patient's unpredictable choices. So, by offering multiple reasonable and safe solutions to her problem, it allowed her to make the decision and be the master of her outcome. By now she was calm and compliant and she chose to allow me to drive her home. I had de-escalated the situation, and everyone went home safe.

That same off-duty officer had afterward thanked me for handling the situation because he was not sure how it was going to end by how distraught and unreasonable she seemed to be acting. It was after that call I realized just how successful de-escalation can be if one simply humbles themselves and at least attempts to employ the tactics. With that being said, I also urge that when employing de-escalation techniques to also remain ready and vigilant to respond accordingly if the situation erupts in a manner where your life, their life, or the lives of others comes into jeopardy.

THE LETTER OF THE LAW V. THE SPIRIT OF THE LAW

"Waste no more time arguing what a good man should be. Be one."

-Marcus Aurelius-
Meditations 10.16

The Royal Ulster Constabulary (RUC) was a controversial British police force in Northern Ireland that was in service from 1922 through 2001. From its inception through its dissolution, the RUC was responsible for police service during a very politically tense and violent time in Northern Ireland that spanned a few decades, known as The Troubles, or more globally known as The Northern Ireland Conflict.

The Troubles started in the 1960s and was a result of a combination of political and religious civil rights protests that were taking place in Northern Ireland at the time, which was then met with alleged violence from the RUC. Northern Ireland civil rights activists then began a campaign and accused the RUC of civil rights violations, police brutality and discrimination. The result of all this then prompted the Provisional Irish Republican Army, (IRA) to wage a war against the RUC in retaliation.

In 1983 approximately 319 RUC police officers were killed, along with another 9,000 being injured or maimed as a result of calculated terrorist-style assassination attempts at the hands of the IRA, making the RUC the most dangerous police force to work for in the world during that time.

In the 1970s, a British Army Officer named Peter Villiers had worked closely with the RUC during the height of the Troubles. Through his experience in the violent world of policing, he began to write and publish books and articles on policing based on his personal reflections as opposed to formal studies. Through his work, he became a Stoic and came to the realization that the virtues of the Stoics are the virtues of a good police officer (the same realization I came to).

In an article I read from Villiers, called *The Police Officer as a Stoic*, he highlighted the four cardinal virtues of the Stoics: wisdom, temperance, courage, and justice, as necessities for being able to practice, what the British call *policing by consent*, but what we call here in the United States, discretion.

He describes policing by consent as a practice that removes the support of policing by authority on which the officer might have otherwise relied and places its major weight upon the shoulders of the individual officer. Basically meaning that it gives the officer the power to police and serve justice in a manner that he/she sees fit and believes in, as opposed to being commanded to police in a certain way in which they might not morally agree with.

Discretion is a phenomenal tool to utilize in the carrying out of lawful duties as long as the officer possesses a moral high ground based around the stoic virtues or any other moral virtues of their belief. Without that moral backbone, the practice of discretion is utterly useless or ignored.

A lack of discretion creates the officer who will recognize when a crime has been committed, regardless of its application to a certain situation, and robotically make arrests. They enforce the exact letter of the law (as it is written on the books) without giving any mind to the spirit of the law (how it applies to a given situation). If this is you, stop being a robot, and start being a human being.

Sometime around 2015, maybe 2016, I was dispatched to a call of a suspicious person riding around a neighborhood on a bicycle. If I remember correctly, the complainant was accusing the suspicious person of riding the exact bicycle that she had reported stolen weeks before.

After canvassing the area for a few minutes looking for this suspicious person, another officer was able to locate him in the immediate area. To skip to the meat of the story, the bike wasn't the one that was stolen. The man ended up being a homeless tinker, who collected scrapped items to pawn for money as a means to make a living.

However, during the course of this encounter, an 18th to 19th-century flint-lock style pistol was found in his possession. When you looked at it, it was questionable whether it was even operable or not. The man was in possession of it with the sole intention of pawning it, as far as he told us, which given the totality of his circumstances, seemed quite plausible.

The primary investigating officer that I was backing-up while querying the man's information for any type of warrants, also ran a criminal history on him and found that he was a convicted felon many years prior. Can you guess what happened next?

To give you a clear background on this officer's style of policing, he was known, and still is for all I know, as "that officer." And I'm sure everyone in law enforcement knows who "that officer" is in their circles. The guy who shows up on calls after everything has calmed down and starts yelling at people and giving lectures, ultimately riling people backup and creating more of a headache than there needed to be. This officer was also the guy that when he did lecture people, he used his pointer finger and shook it at the person as you would see in some 1960's sitcom where a mother would verbally discipline a child. He was quick to arrest at the first sign of any verbal push-back from a person, and relied heavily on a Taser. He, for all intents and purposes, was all ego and no humility. But the funny thing is, it wasn't because he was this huge, bulging guy who could back up his ego, he was maybe 130 pounds soaking wet with a fully equipped duty belt on.

So, to answer the question as to what that officer did next when he found out that the homeless man we were dealing with was a convicted felon, that officer arrested the man for being a convicted felon in possession of a firearm. Given this officer's reputation as being "that officer," I shouldn't have been shocked by this, but I was. Sure, by all means being in accordance with the letter of the law, that officer was completely lawful in his arrest, but in regards to the spirit of the law?

The spirit of the law or law in action is how one applies the law to fit the situation. Basically, utilizing discretion, along with a sense of humility, is considered acting under the spirit of the law.

In the situation where "that officer" arrested the homeless man for being a convicted felon in possession of a firearm over an old, questionably operable flint-lock pistol from the 1800s, seemingly not even loaded with a pellet or gun powder, mixed in with a bunch of other junk that was going to either be trashed or pawned. It was a little ridiculous to me because truthfully, the intent wasn't to "get a dangerous armed felon" off the street along with a "dangerous gun," it was all in the name of feeding that officer's ego and gaining a felony arrest stat, without contemplation of how that frivolous arrest would affect that person's freedom at the moment, as well as farther down the road.

Now, I'm not saying that an action should not have been taken. Of course, in that situation, seizing the gun for destruction and referring the charge to a prosecutor would have been the humbler approach. It would have served the purpose of disarming the felon because in a small glimpse of another reality, could that homeless have used it to commit a violent crime? Absolutely possible, but the totality of the circumstances didn't lean that way in my opinion. And like I said, the intent of the arrest wasn't to serve justice, it was to pad a stat and feed an ego.

I understand that some reading this, may disagree with my assessment of that particular situation, and that's ok. So, I propose another practice I've seen utilized that completely undermines the spirit of the law.

When I was in the field training program at my second agency, I was assigned to an FTO who worked on a squad, who called themselves "the dope squad." Respectfully, that squad did work in a higher drug area than the rest of the majority of the agency, but nonetheless, they proclaimed themselves to be "the dope squad."

One would think that they call themselves that because they make a lot of drug arrests, which they do, but I later saw behind the smoke and mirrors as to how they make drug arrests quantitatively, which in turn is not very qualitative.

During a shift on that squad, we did a lot of proactive policing in the high crime areas with the sole purpose of finding drugs and the fruits that accompany drugs (i.e. guns, knives, burglary tools), which I'm all about. On one particular stop we made, a crack pipe was found on a subject and only a crack pipe. Obviously, the person we found it on was a user, nothing close to resembling what some may define as a "big fish."

My first thought, having been a cop previously and wise enough to give people breaks on paraphernalia, was just to seize it for destruction and move onto actual bigger fish. But instead, I was instructed by my FTO to swab the residue inside the pipe and test it for crack cocaine, and if the test came back positive, which it obviously did, we would be making an arrest for felony possession of a controlled substance, which we obviously ended up doing despite how ridiculous I found it to be.

Again, here is another example of utilizing absolutely no humility and feeding the ego with felony stats to make one feel as if they're truly making a difference. According to the letter of the law, it was allowed and lawful, but the spirit of the law was far from being respected. Ego working at its best. A tactic I swore to never practice again.

It's one thing to be proactive and thorough, and take people to jail that absolutely deserve to go to jail in order to preserve the morals of society, i.e.; an actual dealer with a large amount of drugs; it's another to find any reason whatsoever take someone to jail for something frivolous.

The Stoic Cop: Policing Through Stoic Virtue

What some cops don't care to understand is the long-term impact frivolous arrests can have on a person, specifically destitute individuals. Say you arrest a poor 18-year-old, with no prior history and seemingly respectful demeanor, for a gram of weed just because you can and you want to. They then plea out to a fine which they can't pay, so then a warrant gets issued and/or their license gets suspended. Now they run the risk of getting arrested just for driving because they can't afford to reinstate their license but need to go to work. They eventually get picked up on their warrant, as well as lose their license, lose their job, and the cycle starts all over again and continues.

The point is, we know how to be moral. We know how to utilize discretion. We know how to be good. So, stop letting your ego define what it is to be good in order to rationalize your oppressive decisions. Let your soul define it, let your humility define it. Being a good person comes more naturally that way.

On Being Present

"Being present demands all of us. It's not nothing. It may be the hardest thing in the world to do."

-Ryan Holiday-
Stillness is the Key

It is often said and repeated in the law enforcement profession that people don't call the police because they're having a great fulfilling day; they are calling the police because they're perhaps having the worst day of their life. And this is true.

I can't think of any specific call, probably because there have been too many of them to even remember in detail, but frequently I've answered calls for service for problems that I can't even believe people would call the police for, like trivial neighbor disputes that the two parties are capable of figuring out themselves. And I'm sure you have too.

But it's not your job to screen police phone calls for what your ego believes are real problems, or pick and choose which ones you feel like answering, or which ones are not important at all, because in the grand scheme of things, all of them are important, they are important to the taxpaying citizen who feels that it is important enough to call the police.

What your job entails, despite your perception of their problem, is to utilize humility and be present for the citizen, not just in a physical form, but your mind has to be there as well. People will know right away if you're actually present and listening to their problems when they're explaining them to you. No one likes talking to a wall.

As Ryan Holiday says, being present is probably the hardest thing to do in the world because of all the external distractions and chaos going on around us. For police, it could be multiple people trying to talk to you at once, someone trying to get your attention of the radio, having just dealt with a morally difficult call prior and thinking about that, plus factor in your own personal problems that are on your mind, and you've got a recipe for not being fully present. Despite all that, you need to find the power to tune it out for a brief time and endure it all in order to be present for the citizen before you.

As a police officer, when it comes to being present, do err on the side of caution and utilize the cardinal virtue of temperance. Every situation and person are different. Some situations require more of your attention and presence than others. Beware that being too present can cause you to become too emotionally invested in the situation, and that's not good. Although it is your job to help solve people's problems, it is not your job to bear all the emotional weight of their problems. Bearing the weight of the problems that each and every person you come across throws at you will only drive you off a mental cliff.

So, also remember not to be too detached from being present because then you just come off rough and uninterested, and the citizen is less likely to explain to you in full detail the nature of their problem, which could make your job harder in the long run in trying to solve it.

You need to put yourself in their shoes. How irritating or offensive is it to explain to someone in detail about something big that's going on in your life, but they just don't even make eye contact with you and just nod their heads? It's completely irritating. Remember what the goal is; to solve the problem. You can't solve it if you're not actually there.

On "Thanking Me For My Service"

"When someone is properly grounded in life, they shouldn't have to look outside themselves for approval."

-Epictetus-
Discourses 1.21

We live in a time where self-worth is gauged by how many Instagram followers one has, or how many "likes" one can get from a picture they posted. We place so much mindless value above everything else, on the fact that we are noticed and well-liked by complete strangers all over the world; and police culture is not immune from this fallacy.

I've seen time and time again where officers do a good deed for someone while on duty, film it, and send it out to the world of the social media to see with a catchy hashtag in the hopes of it going viral. Or those cookie-cutter Instagram posts during a holiday where an officer lets everyone know that they are "working so everyone else can enjoy their holiday off," or posting pictures of their scraped elbow showing just how dangerous the job is and how tough they are for having a "boo-boo," and let's not forget to mention those cringey Tik-Tok videos.

But what is the point of all of it? To feed the ego? Those cops want everyone to know that they are doing a public service and they want the praise for doing it. Wrong. That's not public service. That's them doing a personal service with a shallow intent and for the sole purpose of gaining extrinsic value from others that isn't necessary. No one buys it. Most humble cops see right through it, and it's boring.

Some officers may read this and argue, "Well, I'm just trying to humanize the badge." My rebuttal to that is if you want to "humanize" the badge, then go out there in the communities you patrol and be an actual human and not a trendy online persona. Treat people with respect, greet people and have a conversation, go above and beyond for someone without having to let the world know about it.

Sun-Tzu said in his book the *Art of War*:

> "The general who advances without coveting fame and retreats without fearing disgrace, whose only thought is to protect his country and do good service for his sovereign, is the jewel of the kingdom."

It's easy in law enforcement to allow our ego to get us caught up in the need to stand out, be recognized, and receive praise for the work we do by our peers, superiors, and supervisors. We have all, at one point or another, envisioned ourselves as being an absolute hero in the most stressful situation and obtaining fame. We then begin doing good deeds in search of the extrinsic worth we gain from them instead of just doing it for the sake of the good deed because it's the right or humane thing to do.

But all that means is that you are thinking about, and putting yourself first. People may quickly buy into your fame at first, but sooner or later they will see the transparency, they will sense the ego, they will feel the deceit, and the fame will fade just as quickly.

Actions must be selfless. People need to feel and sense the sincerity. Actions done with humility will be overlooked at first, or not even noticed. But, over time they will start to be felt and received wholly by others. That is where deep-rooted and long-lasting respect grows from; selfless actions born from humility. It's a fact that acorns do not grow into oaks overnight, it takes time.

Epictetus lectured in the *Enchiridion* that everyone's actions are driven by self-indulgence. The difference being between the virtuous man and the unvirtuous man is that the unvirtuous man indulges in his own pleasures, wealth, and fame; essentially his vices. While the virtuous man indulges in his loyalty, his discipline, his humility, and whatever other virtue you can fill in here. So, if you must self-indulge, indulge in your virtues.

> *"When you have done a good act and another had received it, why do you look for a third thing besides these, as fools do, either to have the reputation of having done a good act or obtain a return?"*
>
> -Marcus Aurelius-

It's one thing to do a good deed, and have a third-party catch you doing it, film you doing it, and send it out on their own accord. You can't control that, and there is no ego behind it. If anything, that proves that you're doing the job for the right reasons, for the service of others, and not for your own personal fulfillment.

But it's another thing to do the advertising yourself. If you just continue to do good deeds given the nature of your job and affect other people's lives for the better, then that is all the fulfillment you should need, that is where the value of your self-worth should come from.

> *"A man when he has done a good act, he does not call out for others to come and see, but he goes on to another act, as a vine goes on to produce again the grapes in season."*
>
> –Marcus Aurelius-

On Reputation

"Don't let reputation get mixed up with your moral purpose and will power; they are important. Make sure reputation is in the box in the bottom of the drawer marked 'matters of indifference'."

-Vice Admiral James Bond Stockdale-
Courage Under Fire

Law enforcement is a very egotistically driven profession. Everyone at some point in their career has envisioned themselves being the most decorated officer in their agency, with the most accolades, involved in the most heroic actions, and who leaves some sort of lasting legacy in the agency from the reputation they made for themselves. And in the grand scheme things, having a good reputation is, in fact, important to strive for.

A good reputation gives the impression to others that you are of good moral character, that you are hardworking, reliable, trustworthy, easy to supervise or a pleasure to work for, etc. Creating this reputation will allow you to campaign yourself more easily for specialized units and promotional opportunities. But there is always the catch or dichotomy of it. What Vice Admiral Stockdale is saying is not to let the hunt for reputation be at the expense of others or your character, because your character is all that you own and control.

Don't step on the backs of other people to hoist your reputation up. Don't throw someone else out of the way because they were in your way. Basically, don't be a corrupt asshole for the sole purpose of getting ahead of others. Because at the end of your long career, and life for that matter, none of your accomplishments will be remembered by anyone except you.

They are not going to erect a statue of you at HQ. They are not going to rename a street after you. And the longer you're out of the game, the more your name will begin to fade away, and all that will be left is your character.

Remember, reputation is a factor outside our control, and as stoics, we only concern ourselves with what is in our control; our character is in our control. As Marcus Aurelius humbly said:

> *"In a little while you will have forgotten everything, and everything will have forgotten you."*

So, yes, having goals is important, and the best way to achieve your goals is to have a good reputation from being a good person and good coworker. Just don't allow those goals to be the reason you trample others. Don't allow the thoughts of a near unattainable legacy blind you from doing what's proper and moral in the "now."

On Remembering Where You Started

"When you are offended at any man's fault, immediately turn to yourself and quickly reflect in what manner you have erred yourself. For by attending to this you will quickly forget about your anger if you consider that the man is compelled: for what else could he do? Or, if you are able, take away from him the compulsion."

-Marcus Aurelius-
Meditations 10.30

The first agency I worked for had a horrible attrition rate. They couldn't offer enough incentives to keep officers around. The reasons could be written in an entirely different book, but for the sake of brevity, the morale of the agency was just broken for a multitude of reasons. Obviously, I do not work there anymore.

With that being said, it seemed to most other officers at the time, including myself, that the agency was hiring just about anyone in order to put bodies in the ever-increasing number of vacancies in employment. This meant, more often, that the agency was sacrificing quality candidates for quantity, and it was showing. It was getting to the point where recruits were actually failing miserably out of the academy and post-academy type training, and given second, third, and even fourth chances to try and make the cut because the city was that desperate. It was so bad that I can't even remember a time that they actually fired someone who was just not cut out for the job. They retained everyone, it seemed.

There was this one recruit in particular who had come to my precinct. I don't remember hearing how he did in the academy or post-academy training, but since he had been assigned to my precinct to do his field training program, he made quite the reputation for himself. He was a struggler.

One instance in particular, which was one that really damaged his reputation in the eyes of the rest of the officers in the precinct, was a use of force he had gotten into with his field training officer; well, I should say that his field training officer got into and he just stood idly by in shock and panic.

Now, I was not there. I did not witness it. I am going by what the field training officer told me, who had actually been my field training officer at one point, and one that I looked up to the most so I trusted his judgment. He had told me, long story short, that he and this particular recruit had responded to some sort of disturbance call at an apartment complex in one of the many rough sides of town. They had decided to arrest a particular suspect, at which point the suspect resisted and a full-on fight ensued.

The field training officer, along with two other officers who were on scene had been trying to subdue the suspect into handcuffs while getting severely bit by the suspect in the process, all the while this recruit stood there and watched. Never getting involved, never getting on the radio to call for extra assistance, never doing anything. It's also been said that this recruit had a look of shock and fear in his face. Frozen by the shock and failing to act.

This story went all around the precinct. In law enforcement, it's one thing to makes mistakes and screw things up that don't have a lethal or violent outcome, but it's another to make mistakes that jeopardize officer safety, and another to show cowardice. This recruit, in the eyes of the rest of the officers, had sinned.

But nonetheless, he was given extra opportunities to improve and eventually passed field training. And of course, whose shift was he assigned to? The one I was on. And of course, the egotistical part of me hated it. It was also felt with the rest of the guys on the shift just how apprehensive everyone was about him.

He had come to the shift and immediately the tension was felt. No one wanted to ride calls with him, no one wanted him to ride calls with them, and it just escalated from there. He had definitely gotten the hint that no one truly liked him. I mean, there were also other things about his personality that just didn't click as well. He had this way of acting like a know-it-all despite being brand new and having committed a sin in field training. He constantly made rookie mistakes repeatedly and never fixed them. Needless to say, he never really improved in the eyes of the shift.

It had gotten to the point where he approached me one day and inquired as to why everyone disliked him. And of course, I gave it to him straight, perhaps a little too straight with absolutely no chaser behind it. When I think about it now, I didn't handle the situation with any humility at all. It was all ego. And because of that, I missed an important opportunity to guide someone, a fellow officer, who was struggling and actually seeking out help in order to improve himself.

My ego had been too big to be patient enough to explain to him his errors in an understanding fashion. I also never followed any of it up with areas that I thought he was strong at in order to boost his confidence.

I had just blurted out all his weaknesses, as there were quite a few, and left him hanging to deal with it without any helpful explanations. It's no wonder why he never improved. No one, myself included, had the patience or the will to mold him as a teammate should do. After all a shift is a team, and this particular recruit-turned-officer had been exiled by us. We had failed him all because of our egos. We had no humility.

    Why was it that our egos were too big to mentor? Because we forgot how it was to be a rookie and make mistakes. We forgot where we started, and how we got to where we are now. I know I made a lot of mistakes in my beginnings and I still make mistakes today. I try to remember this:

> *"Whenever you are about to find fault with someone, ask yourself the following question: what fault of mine most resembles the one that I am about to criticize?"*
>
>   -Marcus Aurelius-

It falls by the wayside at times sometimes, but we have to remember that everybody starts somewhere just as you did. No one is perfect, and some people learn things at a slower pace than others, so we must be able to find the patience to guide and motivate. So, try to think of it this way:

> *"If a man is mistaken, instruct him kindly and show him his error. But if you are not able, blame yourself, or not even yourself."*
>
>   -Marcus Aurelius-

Meaning, we need to help our new brothers and sisters, just as much as we need to be there and help our current ones. Mentoring new officers ensures they will get up to speed quickly and be an efficient team member. People can't get better if they're ignorant of their weaknesses. If you teach them and they still fail, then you must accept that perhaps it was your method of teaching that failed them and you must reapproach the topic from another angle.

If they still do not get it, then maybe your impression of them as not being cut for the job was right to begin with, and you no longer need to carry the burden of their faults. Perhaps have another person try and help that new officer. See if they have a better angle of approach than you did.

The key is not to ignore the problems or the mistakes the new officer is making. That will compound the issues further. You don't want that new officer teaching even newer officers the wrong information or tactics because no one had ever told him that he was wrong to begin with. Do not let it snowball. Check the ego, take charge, and fix it.

> *"Without an accurate accounting of our own abilities compared to others, what we have is not confidence, but delusion. How are we supposed to reach, motivate, or lead people of we can't relate to their needs because we've lost touch with our own."*
>
> -Ryan Holiday-

Afterthoughts

Ego is one of those aspects of the psyche that if left unchecked can rear its ugly head to the forefront of our personality and wreak havoc on our interpersonal communications. The best remedy to check your ego, well, is to do just that, actually, check and examine your daily actions in order to justify your character. Seneca said it best in a letter to Lucilius:

> *"I shall put myself under observation straight away and undertake a review of my day; a course of which is of the utmost benefit. What really ruins our character is the fact the none of us look back on our life, we think about what we are going to do, and only rarely of that, and fail to think about what we have done, yet any plans for the future are dependent on the past."*
>
> –Letters from a Stoic LXXXIII

In regards to policing, in order to keep your ego and character in check, you should get into the practice of analyzing and debriefing your actions after every call. Ask yourself things like:

Was I shortsighted with a citizen? Did I get frustrated with someone difficult? Did I come off as rude? Did I issue moral justice as my discretion saw fit? Did I make a frivolous arrest to give myself a stat at the expense of someone else's freedom? Did I purposely cut corners?

These are all very important questions to review when you honestly examine yourself. And these questions deserve and require an honest answer if you wish to achieve the point of the exercise which is to keep your ego and character in constant check. Any deviation from the honest truth is detrimental to your character; ego is essentially winning the fight at that point.

Furthermore, when you do answer those questions honestly and come to the conclusion that your character needs work, what is the game plan to fix it? Recognizing the character flaw is half the battle, the other half is fixing it, so make sure that you are doing that as well.

Humility is a skill that I've found to be extremely useful when implemented correctly in the field. Being humble and utilizing humility isn't a weakness, it's a strength. I'm not saying that you have to play patty cakes with everyone you come into contact with, or be officer friendly who always sees the good in people while naively never sensing the bad. That is a lethal recipe. What I am saying though is that you will have more success in building relationships and gaining compliance from people when you humble yourself, listen rather than talk or command, and have a general sense of empathy for other people's problems. At the same time, also utilize vigilance. It's possible to appear friendly, unthreatening and understanding while still having a lethal guard up that the other person doesn't become intimidated by.

Citizen interactions aside, remember that it is also important to be humble towards fellow officers. It doesn't matter if you're a full-time SWAT operator, a School Resource Officer (SRO), or anything in between. Every single position is an integral part of the mission of your agency and the profession. Walking around with a chip on your shoulder because you made X amount of felony arrests versus someone else with Y amount of misdemeanor arrests is arbitrary. It means nothing in the long run except for making you look like an asshole.

In the book *Deadly Beat,* ex-RUC police constable Richard Latham, found himself in a predicament during an armed robbery investigation. While taking his report and airing over the radio the description of the suspect, he had heard from undercover units that they were tailing a possible suspect on foot through the busy city streets of Belfast, heading right back towards the scene of the crime. The suspect apparently had a black trench coat on with what appeared to be a concealed firearm underneath which was later confirmed visually.

The predicament came when constable Latham had visual on the suspect and could see him walking right towards him. Thoughts began to run through his mind on whether to draw down on the suspect or not. If he drew down, he risked having a shootout in the busy streets of Belfast, with many innocent people in the backdrop behind his target, as well as many innocent people in between him and his target. He had to think quickly about how he was going to engage the suspect.

As the suspect got relatively close, constable Latham ultimately decided that tackling and wrestling the suspect into submission with the aid of other officers was the best approach, and in the end, was successful. The suspect was arrested, a gun removed off of the street, and no one was hurt in the process.

Latham then went on to describe that even though he received praise from his chain-of-command, it was not long before more of the egotistical officers questioned his judgments. He reflected on how many of the officers not involved in the situation suddenly became firearms experts, and all became brave decisive officers who knew exactly what should have been done had it been them in his shoes.

That right there is a huge issue in the police world, not only do we have our decisions second-guessed by civilians and the media, but we also have to suffer the critique of our fellow officers. And the root of it is because of ego. If you read this and recognize that you are one of those officers, stop.

Be diplomatic in your interactions with co-workers. Don't sit around and talk shit when someone makes a mistake, don't ignore a bad tactic another officer consistently makes because it makes you look better, or don't expect a rookie to go out on the streets after training and be completely up to speed. Show humility, guide the struggling rookie up to speed, show the officer with bad tactics a better way, and lift that officer up who made a mistake instead of kicking them when they are down. It won't be long before you find yourself in the same position, under the microscope, being scrutinized, and hoping that no one is going to think less of you.

PART II

Vigilance

"All the terms of our human lot should be before our eyes; we should be anticipating not merely all that commonly happens but all that is conceivably capable of happening, if we do not want to be overwhelmed and stuck numb by rare events as if they were unprecedented ones; fortune needs comprehending in a thoroughly comprehensive way."

-Seneca-
Letters from a Stoic CXI

General James Mattis of the United States Marine Corps was well-known amongst his peers as an intellectual with a quiet demeanor; a scholar of war and strategy. Stemming from humble beginnings in Washington state, he grew up in a household that placed an emphasis on reading books rather than watching mindless television, to the point where his parents didn't even keep a television in the house, which helped mold him into the forward thinker he became as one of the highest-ranking leaders in one of the world's strongest militaries.

Across the United States military, he was known to have practiced humility, completely not above interacting with even the most junior of enlisted men and women despite his high rank. He was a well-versed tactician in strategy, history, leadership, politics, and above all, war; coming to be known as the *warrior-scholar*.

Another known, but perhaps lesser-known fact about General Mattis, was his practice of stoicism. General Mattis has stated to an audience at the Virginia Military Institute that Marcus Aurelius' *Meditations* is a must-read for every American citizen, even admitting to carrying a copy of the book on his person during deployments as a way to keep a sense of stillness in the midst of chaos.

Even 1,000 years before the existence of Emperor Marcus Aurelius and 2,500 years before General Mattis, there reigned another philosophical warrior; one whose teachings have also stood the test of time in the realm of strategy and tactics. I am talking about the Chinese general and war strategist: Sun-Tzu. He philosophized on aspects of war that he compiled into 13 different important areas and into what is known as the book, *The Art of War*.

The very first line out of the book Sun-Tzu is quoted as saying:

"Warfare is the greatest affair of state, the basis of life and death, the Way (Tao) to survival or extinction. It must be thoroughly pondered and analyzed."

Realizing the importance, responsibility, and gravity of war, as well as the fragility it brings to the existence of life, Sun-Tzu had the insight to know that war is something to be studied and analyzed in order to understand the "why" and the purpose of it.

"Let no act be done without a purpose, nor otherwise according to the perfect principles of art."
–Marcus Aurelius-

Without understanding the "why" of war, there is an ignorance to the repercussions of it, there is an ignorance to the mortality of it, and an ignorance to its devastation of civilization. Understanding the "why" of war keeps one vigilant and in tune with its severity.

Sun-Tzu realized it 2,500 years ago, and General Mattis realizes it today that being a student of history, philosophy, and war instills the virtue of vigilance in one's life; the ability to be keenly watchful in one's demeanor in order to detect danger as it comes with the preparedness to combat it and persevere. General Mattis said it best:

"Be polite, be professional, but have a plan to kill everyone you meet."

Comparing law enforcement with war to the average citizen may seem crass and obtuse, but it's important to point out that war isn't just blood, carnage, and savagery as one thinks of when they hear the word *war*. The idea of war, along with its strategies, tactics, and philosophies can be applied to many facets of life. Jocko Willink has even gone as far as to say in his podcast that "war is life."

In fact, the first time I picked up *The Art of War* and read it was when I was training in mixed martial arts. I had a coach at the time who was a Marine, as well as an Olympic caliber Greco-Roman wrestler. He had been brought in by our head coach to teach aspects of Greco-Roman wrestling that would strengthen our skills. I remember going to the very first wrestling class where he assumed his position as the wrestling coach. The class had completed its routine warm-up drills: running, jumping rope, stretching, etc.

He then had us all gather around in a circle where I had thought he would immediately begin teaching us moves or demonstrating some drills we were going to implement in order to ease us into a specific move we would eventually be doing later on. But instead, the coach told us all to have a seat, and then pulled out of his gym bag, an old beat-up notebook that had scribbles and highlights inside of it.

As he began reading, it was obvious that he was reading his philosophies and wisdom about wrestling that he had compiled over the years. We literally did not do any drilling that entire session. He simply lectured, with absolute passion, his philosophy, his wisdom, and theories about how to approach the sport.

Now, I will mention at this point that I grew up wrestling since I was 5 years old. Over the years, I've had countless instructors and coaches from vast camps and seminars that I attended, and this coach was the only one who had taken the time, an entire training session, to discuss the philosophy and wisdom of wrestling. It was actually inspiring.

During his coach's time in the Marines, he had read the *Art of War* and realized that its philosophies also paired well with his wrestling. As he recommended the book to everyone, he also mentioned that it could be applied to every aspect of one's life: business, school, politics, etc. And after reading it, I saw that he was right. I applied the book to mixed martial arts, just as I am now applying it to law enforcement.

For law enforcement, war can come in many forms: the internal emotional/mental war one endures in their lives, the war to get ahead at their job, the war of interacting with difficult people, and even the actual war of engaging with an armed subject.

The Stoic Cop: Policing Through Stoic Virtue

Police officers deal with all types of war on a daily basis. The only reason I compare law enforcement with war is because to most, it can feel that way at times, but also because a lot of ancient philosophers use metaphors of war in their writings to compare to life's daily struggles. After all, war is life, right? Take Seneca for example when he said:

> *"I may wish to be free from torture, but if the time comes for me to endure it, I'll wish to bear it courageously with bravery and honor. Wouldn't I prefer not to fall into war? But, if war does befall me, I'll wish to carry nobly the wounds, starvation and other necessities of war."*

Seneca was a politician for most of his life and probably never saw a battlefield, but he uses war as a metaphor for the worst possible conditions, and how to realize that although you don't wish for war, you must prepare yourself and remain vigilant to endure it to the best of your ability.

Vigilance is important because it balances out humility. Over-implementing humility can make you naïve to the bad-natured individuals that lurk out in society, make you complacent to the fact that there are wolves out there who want to take their shot at you, and blind you to danger that you should see coming.

This is why I followed up humility with vigilance, and why I opened this part of the book with General Mattis' quote. As important as it is to practice humility, it's also important to realize that a *yes* person can easily and quickly become a *no* person, at which time you must meet violence with a higher level of violence if you wish to live to see another day.

In order to obtain supreme vigilance, you must be vigilant in three areas: mentally, physically and emotionally. It is not enough to concentrate on one or two areas and be deficient in one. It is like a tripod; a tripod needs all three legs to stand erect. If one goes down, the whole thing comes down. You can mentally prepare yourself all you want for a fight, but if you physically can't keep up in the fight, it's not going to do you any good. Just the same that you can prepare yourself physically for a fight, but if you haven't humbled yourself in the process or meditated on your mortality, you're asking to be emotionally hurt if you find yourself on the losing end of a fight. With any endeavor in life, it is always best to be well-rounded.

Training

"If you want a man to keep his head when crisis comes, you must give him some training before it comes."

-Seneca-
Letters from a Stoic XVIII

Before diving into the different levels of vigilance, an issue needs to be addressed. An issue that is important and, above all, the conduit to achieving proficiency in all areas of vigilance. It is the fundamental cornerstone which reveals a reference point that allows you to know exactly how you will respond to the chaos of a crisis when the time comes to act, as well as where one sets a benchmark to improve upon each and every session so that you do not lose your nerve when the urgency strikes. And this seems to be the thing cops like to complain about probably more than anything: *training*.

The worst part about it is that most officers complain even though they may only train once a year during some sort of annual in-service or in-house training. Why is that? How is it that performing a task which can only make them better, even if it is on a measly one-week-a-year basis, could possibly stress them out that much? I see it all the time, the officer who stands off to the side, goes through the motions, makes excuses as to why they suck or can't perform an exercise, complains about the heat, complains about being bored, claims they don't need to train anymore, etc. And it's usually the out of shape, or senior/ranking officers who feel like they've "been there and done that," or say that "it's repetitive." Do you feel that you fall into this category of officers?

Let's think about it and break it down: you get a week off from working the streets where you have to solve other people's problems, engage in real-life high-stress incidents, and potentially put your life at risk. The tradeoff for training is a laid back (in-service is always laid back), slowed down training environment while still getting paid the same.

The best part about it is that you can actually learn and take away new tactics, ideas, tools, skills, and knowledge that can enrich your job performance as long as you strive to gain something out of it. Even if it is repetitive stuff you've gone over before, it is always good to refresh, recalibrate, remember, and retain all that old information.

Complaints aside though, let's be honest, police don't train enough, and that is a sad truth. Between calls for service never stopping, personnel shortages, limited budgets for ammo and other training supplies, etc., training can be hard to even come by. And it's because of this lack of training that mistakes are made out on the street which leads to society acknowledging the fact that police aren't trained enough.

Now, I will say that in the academy, as well as post-academy based training, the amount of training repetitions is phenomenal, but where the problem begins to show itself is when we don't keep up with our training. Specialized skills tactics can be hard to master, but very easy to forget if not routinely practiced.

If you can't train at work, then you must train elsewhere. Dry fire your weapons at home, practice reloading your mags, repetitively clear your own house, etc. Along with police tactics, you must also train your body, as well as your mind. You have to keep up with your physical fitness, eat relatively healthy, stay up to date on the ever-changing verbiage of the law, and even study philosophy as you are now.

Training in all aspects, even for an hour a day, will keep you fresh, prepared and ready, and hungry to take on all of the chaos that can be thrown your way at any time in the course of your duty. Don't be the officer who sits in the back of the class and makes sarcastic slights the entire time at the expense of your own boredom or disdain for the topic, don't be the officer who makes up an injury to avoid any type of physical-based training. It's detrimental to you, detrimental to the other officers who rely on you to be ready to act when the crisis comes, and detrimental to the citizen who has called upon you to act and intervene in life-threatening scenarios. What use will you be to anyone if your mind and body are untrained? The answer is not any good at all; you will most likely not meet the expectations needed to be successful, or worse you will fail to act.

Take for example Deputy Scot Peterson, formerly of the Broward County Sheriff's Office, during the Margery Stoneman Douglas High School Shooting in Parkland, FL. He was seen in surveillance footage from a camera positioned on the exterior of the school, failing to act for not entering the school building while seventeen (17) students were massacred and another 17 more injured at the hands of a mass shooter. Due to his failed actions, he was subsequently arrested and charged with child neglect, culpable negligence, and perjury. During an interview with Today Show host Savannah Guthrie, Peterson stated that he thought what he was hearing was possibly firecrackers and not gunshots.

Can someone, who is supposed to be adequately trained, truly mistake the sound of high caliber gunfire inside of a building at close proximity for firecrackers? Can someone who is vigilant mentally, emotionally, and physically freeze up as he appeared to have done? My opinion is that it's not very likely. And also, as a result of the shooting and Deputy Peterson's failed actions, former Broward County Sheriff Scott Israel was relieved of his position by Florida Governor Ron

DiSantis for failing to properly train his deputies for active shooter scenarios.

With all that being said, and despite your stance on the subject matter, the Parkland Shooting foreshadows how inadequate training in a high liability profession has the potential to be catastrophic when one fails to act accordingly. So, I urge all who read this, and to all who hate training, to keep the Parkland Shooting, former Deputy Peterson, and former Sheriff Israel in mind when you even begin to think about complaining, or choosing to half-ass a training drill. It could cost you your job, your freedom, and above all the lives of innocent victims.

Mental Vigilance

"Begin the morning by saying to yourself, I shall meet with the busybody, the ungrateful, arrogant, deceitful, envious, and unsocial. All these things happened to them by reason of their ignorance of what is good and evil. But I, who have seen the nature of good that is beautiful, and of the bad that is ugly, and the nature of him who does wrong, that it is akin to me, not only for the same or seed, but that it participates in the same intelligence and same portion of the divinity, I can neither be injured by any them, for no one can fix on me what is ugly, nor can I can be angry with any of my kinsman."

-Marcus Aurelius-
Meditations 2.1

Anyone who's ever played a sport has probably heard the ratio tossed around on the application of mental preparedness v. physical preparedness: it being eighty (80) percent mental and twenty (20) percent physical. I personally have always found that to be relatively accurate. The triumph over any game, match, battle, obstacle, problem, puzzle, etc.

in life all starts with some sort of planning or preparation, implemented with mental vigilance.

> "This then, is the beginning of philosophy, an awareness of one's own mental fitness."
>
> –Epictetus-

Mental vigilance is the knowledge that one gains in order to internally prepare the mindset one needs to recognize and detect unforeseen problems that need to be addressed. This is the mental state a cop needs to prepare for the stress they are bound to encounter, accompanied with the understanding they cannot control any of it, only how they will react to it. The best way that I know to sharpen mental vigilance is as simple as being a student of history. Machiavelli had that notion 500 years ago when he said in *The Prince*:

> "To exercise the intellect the prince should read histories, and study there the actions of illustrious men, to see how they have born themselves in war, to examine the causes of their victories and defeat, so as to avoid the latter and imitate the former."

History is the building block and foundation for maintaining mental vigilance. History gives you a glimpse into the victories and losses that people before you have endured, and how they arrived at those victories or losses. And as we all know, history repeats itself, so it is almost like being able to see into the future if you really think about it. Seeing someone else in history make a mistake and the consequences that became of it is the ultimate tool for your mental vigilance.

So, when it comes to making mistakes or experiencing failures, this is how you need to start looking at things: any mistake you have ever made, was made by someone else at some point in time. If you study history, then you'll know how someone else responded to it. If they responded well, then you'll know exactly what to do. If they responded poorly, then you'll know exactly what not to do, and you'll be able to properly formulate your own, better response to the situation.

Learning from your own mistakes is a good way to gain mental vigilance, but learning from other people's mistakes is a better way to gain mental vigilance. Learning from your own means that you already had to make a mistake because you were ignorant of some sort of fact or notion of the act you committed. But learning from someone else's mistake means that you saw how their fates played out firsthand, and now you have the knowledge to not make that mistake yourself. It truly is a crystal ball if you utilize the knowledge of history as such.

So, why is that there are people out there who tend to still consciously make those same mistakes? Take for example the deadly sin of *complacency*. From day one in the academy, we have all heard the phrase, *complacency kills*, and yet there are still officers all over the world who succumb to complacency; because they're not being disciplined enough to learn from history and utilize mental vigilance.

We are taught that hands are the deadliest appendages on a human. If you can't see a person's hands, then you have to be vigilant enough to assume that there is a weapon in it. Any easement away from that assumption will cause you to react slowly if there is ever a situation when there is a weapon.

I remember one particular call I rode where being on point with my mental vigilance probably saved my partner and myself from a potentially lethal situation. It was a report of a sex crime. Most victims who report any type of sex crime usually don't report them immediately. Either a few hours or a few days may go by before they come forward, and a suspect is usually long gone.

So, this one particular night, I received this call for a report of a sex crime. It was reported that the suspect was still on scene, which immediately stimulated my mental vigilance. When I arrived on the scene I practiced all basic tactics: turning off my headlights on the street of the dispatched location, parking a few houses down the road, approaching the house on foot, and meeting the victim outside. The victim had confirmed that the assailant was still inside the house.

Once a back-up officer had arrived on scene, it was decided that we would approach the house and make contact with this alleged suspect. I began to approach the front door of the house, but immediately thought it better to approach a different door because if the suspect knew we were there, they would anticipate us trying to make contact at the front door; and if they wanted to go down fighting, they probably would have set up some sort of a defense on the front door.

So, we tried a side door that ended up being ajar. I stood to the side of the threshold of the door on the outside and proceeded to push the door open to see in. The doorway entered into the kitchen, and it was a straight shot forward from there into the living room. So, from the outside of the side door, I could see most of the kitchen and all the way into the living room where I observed a male, nonchalantly sitting in a recliner chair, and rocking back and forth almost like he had been waiting for us to talk to him. The recliner chair was perpendicular to my line of sight, so all I could see was the right side of his body.

Still standing outside the threshold of the door off to the side, I made myself known to him in order to get his attention, and he acknowledged me from his recliner chair. I told him that I needed to speak with him in regards to the allegations, at which time he had invited me inside his house. I began to step through the threshold and simultaneously asked him if he had an ID anywhere. The suspect, with almost a delightful tone in his voice, said he did and at the same time began to reach down to his left side towards the floor where I had no line of sight.

Immediately, aware that he was reaching to an area that I could not see, I began to un-holster my weapon. The suspect, seeing my reaction, immediately placed his hands up and realized that he shouldn't have been reaching for anything. We then had the suspect get up out of his recliner, and conducted the field interview from his kitchen table. Prior to that I had quickly checked the floor on to the left side of the recliner but did not see any weapons at that time.

To shorten the story, detectives had gotten search warrants signed for the residence and a search was executed. Under the recliner towards the left side, a revolver was found. Not to mention the front of the recliner was facing the front door of the residence where I had originally begun to walk up to. It totally makes you think what the suspect's intentions were.

My thought is that he knew that he had committed a pretty egregious crime and had nowhere to go, so he had probably made the decision to sit in his recliner near the front door with a handgun and wait for our arrival. It also makes you think, what if I had decided to stick with the front door like originally planned, and didn't have the mental vigilance to realize that was a bad idea? What if I didn't have the mental vigilance to recognize that when I asked for his ID, he began to reach towards an area that I could not see? What if I had decided to be complacent that night?

In hindsight, that suspect had a plan, and I was able to recognize it because I was mentally vigilant. I had been taught proper tactics for approaching a house, as well as learned about scenarios where officers had been killed in the line of duty because they were lax with their tactics because they got complacent. And those are just basic lessons. Imagine how much more sound you could be in your tactics if you continue to review cases and scenarios where officers are killed in some more complex scenarios?

Always stay a student of history. Study victorious times in history, as well as catastrophic times in history.

> *"A wise man ought always to follow the paths beaten by great men, and to imitate those who have been supreme, so that if his ability does not equal theirs, at least it will savor of it."*
>
> *–Niccolo Machiavelli-*

Physical Vigilance

"Be upright, or be made upright."

-Marcus Aurelius-
Meditations 7.12

The second area of vigilance one must be proficient in is physical vigilance; the physical preparedness one has that affords the insight to recognize their physical abilities, as well as limitations when urgency strikes. This is the readiness to place an immense amount of stress on the heart, joints, muscles, and bones at any moment, and your body's ability to respond well to that stress and actually work when you need it the most. In order to obtain that readiness, you must introduce your body to a certain level of good physical stress on a regular and routine basis. You must also avoid introducing stress that will affect your body negatively or adversely.

You can't be 300 pounds, eating McDonald's every day because it's free, and never work out, and expect to able to chase down a fleeing criminal in a foot chase. Well, some of those types of cops actually don't expect to chase fleeing suspects down, they rely a lot on the hopes that a K-9 unit will track their suspects down for them. But the cops who do live that lifestyle and actually do try to run down suspects on foot are the same ones we read about in the news who die of a heart attack while on duty.

You can't be the gun enthusiast who knows the nomenclature to every gun ever made and can shoot the bullseye of a target a mile away, or the officer who thinks that the Taser is the great equalizer of any fight, or the person who has never taken a self-defense class or even taken defensive tactics seriously and expect to be any good in a fight. This is police work. Most violent encounters will be close combat, so the need to place so much focus on shooting targets accurately a mile away is counterproductive. The Taser is just a tool that is bound to malfunction or fail, so relying on it too much instead of taking the time to take defensive tactics seriously is a detriment to you. As Epictetus said:

> *"Don't put your purpose in one thing and expect to see progress elsewhere."*

Meaning, in regards to these examples, don't place all your reliance on one specific skill or outside resources and expect to be a well-rounded cop because once that one skill or those outside resources are gone or fail, all you have is yourself. K-9 units are not always going to be available or successful, Tasers will not always work, the chances of getting into a long-range gun battle are slim, and the chances on close-quarter combats is supremely real.

So, honestly ask yourself this, when all the support systems you rely on fail, will your body be able to fill in the gaps? Will you have other skills in your bank to cash in on? Will your body respond the way you need it to and endure the stress, absorb injury, and persevere?

Or will your heart give out on you, will your lungs die out quickly, will your muscles fatigue, will your joints seize up, will you have no other skill to rely on? If you answered honestly that you know your body will not respond as you need it to, then you are severely lacking in physical vigilance. If you want your body to work, you need to start training it.

We've already established that the plan to overcome any obstacle is 80 percent mental and 20 percent physical, but what we haven't established yet, and which is the big elephant in the room, is that mental preparation is the easy part. Being physically vigilant, although the lesser part of the game plan is always the harder part of the game plan. This is because anyone can sit back and relax, watch a motivating movie, listen to a motivating speech, read a motivating book, and conjure up all the ways in which they plan to be better, and which they will implement…starting tomorrow. Then tomorrow comes, and only a fraction of people will actually put their newfound confidence and goals into action.

And it's true, physical exertion and stress is hard, it can be painful, it can be debilitating, but if you had prepared your body in advance to endure the exertion, then the suck factor would decrease, the pain wouldn't be as sharp, and you wouldn't feel as debilitated. On the other hand, you have to start somewhere, you have to rip the Band-Aid off and endure the initial pain and soreness that comes when beginning a physical training regiment, and the time to start is always going to be *now*.

As I mentioned before, being physically vigilant also encompasses the knowledge of recognizing your limitation and skill level. Even Socrates, culturally regarded as the wisest man in human history, had the inclination 2,500 years ago to realize the that we must experience what our bodies are capable of when he was remembered by his student Xenophon as saying:

> *"No man has the right to be an amateur in the matter of physical training. It is a shame for a man to grow old without seeing the beauty and strength the body is capable of."*

So, be smart and utilize the virtue of temperance. Don't go out there on day one and try to run a marathon and squat 500 pounds. Your body will respond negatively, if at all, to those demands. Like every metaphor you've ever heard in regards to building a structure, you must first build a solid foundation before you begin to build upwards. It's just common sense.

If you set the intensity too hard too fast, you're just asking to get injured, or you'll be so sore that you'll discourage yourself from continuing on with your training cycle. Find and feel for where your physical threshold is, and work to do just a little more than that. Always continue to step just beyond that threshold, but make sure not to launch yourself through it; just inch through it instead.

When planning your training cycle, make sure to recognize what your goals are. If it's to have more endurance, then run; if you want to be stronger, then lift weights; if you want to learn how to defend yourself better in a fight, find yourself a gym that teaches self-defense and specifically ones that cater to police defensive tactics. The goal should be to be well-rounded in all these areas, but if you're already proficient in one area, it would probably be best to start concentrating on another. Again, common sense.

Also, think of the skills and functions you will physically need to perform the job of a police officer. This is where utilizing mental vigilance comes into play. If you've been studying history and mentally planning as you should, then you would have prepared yourself to know what skills have either worked for you in the past when you were physically capable and what skills have worked for others. When you realize which skills and functions that you need to exercise, begin to train them.

I remember when I first got into law enforcement and entered into the police academy, I was still in mixed martial arts shape from when I was training for fights. My overall physical fitness was very well-rounded; I had great lung and muscular endurance, above-average absolute strength (maximal strength regardless of your size), incredible relative strength (maximal strength in regards to your size), and was decently fast. I was physically ahead of the rest of my academy class from the beginning, and maintained my physical lead throughout, ultimately receiving the top physical fitness award at graduation.

Throughout the academy and immediately afterward, my workouts consisted of a circuit-based training regimen that focused on fitness functionality. I would go down to the park close to my home where they had a 1.5-mile track aligned with workout stations every 50 yards or so. I would run that track and stop at stations that consisted of pull-ups and leg raises, declined sit-ups, different angled push-ups, jump squats, etc. I would try to do as many reps of each exercise as I could at each station and then continue on with the run around the track, and I ultimately did two laps around the track, making my run three miles intermittent AMRAPs of exercises. On some days I would try to incorporate some sort of sprint, but admittedly, I hate sprints and in hindsight, realistically didn't incorporate them as much as I should have.

Needless to say, when I finally hit the streets both on FTO and solo status, I was in tip-top shape, able to chase down suspects on foot and hop 6-foot fences with ease in full gear. And for those reading who are not police officers, duty belts with a handgun, two to three fully loaded magazines, a Taser, a baton, and preferably two sets of handcuffs can add a weight of roughly 20-30 lbs. to your person, so being able to run and jump fences easily does take some good athleticism.

As the years went on, the fitness goals in my personal life shifted. I no longer did any circuit training, long-distance running, sprints, or any other type of exercise that would improve my functionality as a whole. Instead, I had my eyes set on powerlifting. Now, obviously powerlifting is great for absolute strength, explosiveness, and even mobility when programmed properly, but the other side of powerlifting involved a great deal of eating. More calories equal more energy which equals greater strength output during training sessions.

Over the course of three years or so that I competitively trained for powerlifting, I had put on around thirty pounds of muscle, as well as fat. I went from an average height, yet physically fit, 175 pounder to a wide 205 pounder at my heaviest. And although my absolute strength had flourished, what I didn't realize was how much my endurance and relative strength suffered.

It wasn't until one shift where I had demanded my body perform a certain way and it failed on me in a manner that I had never experienced before. Long story short, the driver of a stolen vehicle had fled from a traffic stop of another officer and ended up crashing in the immediate area I was patrolling. I got to the scene first and found that the occupants had fled from the vehicle. A K-9 unit then arrived on scene and we began tracking the suspects once a perimeter had been set up.

We had run/tracked across this open field that was about 50-75 yards in length. 50-75 yards doesn't sound long or even that hard to run, and it had never been hard for me before, but at that moment in the physical state I was in (unrealized to me at that time), I was pretty tired after running it.

Of course, after having just run that open field, our first immediate obstacle was a wooden, 6-foot privacy fence with the outside of the panels facing us, meaning that the brace usually in the middle of the fence to hold it together and support it, was on the other side of the fence, so there was nothing to step up on as a boost. But at that point in time, I wasn't fazed by it because I had hopped fences many times in full gear with no problem.

The K9 officer had lifted his dog over the fence first, he then launched himself over the fence easily, followed by me; except I was not getting over the fence. I had jumped, grabbed the top of the fence and began to pull myself up, and tried kicking my legs over, but I had no relative strength to get myself over. I had my head over the fence and could see the K9 officer and his dog waiting for me on the other side. It was embarrassing.

I then tried a second time. This time with a running start. I ran, jumped up, grabbed the top of the fence, pulled myself up, and tried walking my feet up, but could not get any traction. So, I tried again to throw my legs up and over but failed a second time; noticing that the other officer and his dog were still waiting on me while the suspects got further and further away. I attempted the same thing a third time, the only difference was that this time, as I had my head over the fence, I could see the officer and his dog running ahead without me.

As humiliated as I felt, it was also motivational. I gave it a fourth attempt, with everything I had in me and was finally successful. Eventually, I caught up with the K9 officer and his dog and we were successful in finding the two suspects from the stolen vehicle. It was a win in the end, but needless to say, I was still angry and upset with myself.

Never had my body not been able to perform when I needed it to, never had another officer given up on me because I couldn't perform the job, and never had I felt so embarrassed in the course of my career.

I went home later and really thought about what had happened. First thing first, I to check my ego and humble myself in order to be able to analyze honestly. To reiterate Epictetus' insight again:

> *"Don't put your purpose in one thing and expect to see progress elsewhere."*

And that is exactly what I did; I placed all my efforts and purpose into becoming big and strong while neglecting all other aspects of physical fitness and expected that I still would have maintained all those other areas. I realized that I had strayed away from running and other athletically functional exercises, as well as sacrificed a moderate diet in the name of strength. I had created the chaos I felt because I lost control of my perception of what was important in the realm of physical fitness.

Now, I understand that being a competitive powerlifter I should have been able to pull myself up and over that fence without too much strain, which I ultimately did, but I can't fully explain just how hard it was for me. It had never been that hard in my life. My ignorance of other areas of fitness that I had once been strong in made me unaware of my newfound limitations and weaknesses.

Having that moment of realization, needless to say, I had to incorporate exercises into my training regimen that would guide in making sure I never had an issue pulling myself up over a fence again. So, what did I do? A lot of weighted pull-ups. I picked an exercise that simulated the function of jumping a fence and chipped away at it. So, getting back to my point, realize what physical functionality you are weak at, find an exercise that simulates it, and put in the work.

The next thing to do is to make sure you're also paying attention to your recovery. General muscle soreness is normal and a part of training but still listen to your body, if you're beginning to actually hurt while performing a specific exercise, either lighten up the intensity or weight, stop doing that exercise and find an alternative one that serves a similar function but gets rid of the pain; if it is really bad, stop doing exercises that concentrate of that specific part of your body and alter your workout to another concentration. As the old adage goes: "improvise, adapt, and overcome."

Pushing through *the hurt* isn't optimal training; that will only get you injured. And what good are you at work if you are injured? The whole point of physical vigilance is to prepare and ready your body for performance, not beating it up until it's unable to perform.

Last area to cover, which is probably the hardest part in implementing physical vigilance more than the actual physical training itself; diet. Besides lack of job related training, or lack of physical training, or the copious amounts of emotional stress police take on, the most detrimental vice that plagues a police officer's well-being may very well be their diet or lack thereof.

Poor diets add unnecessary fat, increase blood pressure, clog arteries, onset diabetes, affect the function of the heart, affect essential hormone levels which affect emotional behaviors, decrease energy, increase stress levels, and the list can absolutely go on. But why do we eat so poorly?

A large part of poor dieting does result from stress eating. Humans are known to pacify negative feelings and emotions through foods that bring them comfort, that briefly stimulate those serotonin receptors in the brain, and give them momentary relief from stress. But that is just what it is, momentary.

Stress eating may comfort you initially and bring emotional relief, but it is such a short relief. It lasts probably just as long as it takes you to actually consume the food, and once you're done, the joy is gone and you're right back to where you were prior to the cupcake you just ate. Although your intention was to pacify the emotional stress, what you really did was fail in the discipline to avert from your negative desires of which you have control over.

Some of what Epictetus taught in order to achieve happiness revolved around the battle between your aversions and desires.

> *"Remember that desire promises the chance of reaching what you desire, and that aversion promises to not fall into that which you averse; that he who fails to reach the object of his desire is unfortunate, and that he who falls into the object of his aversion, is unhappy."*

Meaning that if we desire a goal and do not achieve it, we will be unhappy; if we avoid a certain situation and still fall into it, we will also be unhappy. His approach to fixing this battle was this when it comes to desires:

> *"Let go of all desire for the moment: for if you desire what is not in our control, you will surely be unfortunate, and of the things that are within our control, how great they may be, nothing is yet in your possession."*

Meaning that you should exercise caution with your desires. First, analyze what the desire is. Is the desire in your control? If you desire something that you've established you have control over (in regards to the topic at hand, having a good diet) then you should go after that desire. Next, is the desire a vice? If the desire is a vice (eating a cupcake) then you should exercise more caution, not that you should avert it completely because cupcakes are delicious, but ask yourself if you've earned it; honestly earned it.

If you desire something not in your control (winning the lottery) than those desires should actually be placed into your aversions. And when it comes to winning over your aversions, Epictetus said:

> "Only have aversion towards the things that are unnatural and in your control, you will never fall into the object of your aversion. But if you have aversion towards sickness, death or poverty, you will be unhappy. Therefore, take away your aversion to all the things that are not in our control and transfer it to the things that are unnatural and in our control."

Meaning that if you have an aversion to something that is in your control (eating a cupcake) then you should succeed in averting/avoiding it (implemented with discipline), but if you have an aversion to something not in your control, his example of death, then you will obviously panic when it hangs near.

So, to get back to the original point, eating poorly is undoubtedly within your control, so there is no excuse to fail in it. Eating optimally is also in your control and should be a desire. It is all a matter of perception.

Another reason cops eat so poorly is because of convenience. Sometimes meals have to be sacrificed when urgency strikes, so a lot of the times fast food is the most convenient way to scoff down some food on the go. Not to mention, a lot of fast-food restaurants offer discounts to cops quite frequently, and other enticing incentives to eat poorly. Again, win the battle with your aversion and desires. Realistically, as a cop, you should avert receiving promised discounts to begin with, and you should avert things proven to be bad for you.

Try meal prepping and bringing food to work. It sets you up for *on-the-go* eating, as well as, takes away the urge to eat out. But, if you must eat out, there are places out there that offer quality food. They may be more in price, but it's the price you pay to maintain your physical vigilance. A last option is to practice intermittent fasting. Fast while you're at work and have eating periods at home.

To go back to the beginning of this chapter and drive the point of physical vigilance home, I quote Marcus again:

"Be upright, or be made upright."

Physical vigilance means being upright when it matters most. The only time you should be made upright is during training. If someone is imposing their will on you and making you upright in the streets, it's because you weren't vigilant with your physical fitness, you weren't training the essential functions of your body, you were complacent in thinking you could act when you couldn't. Don't wait until you're in the fight for your life to realize your limitations. Realize them in training and strive to expand them past the limitations of potential enemies.

Emotional Vigilance

> *"In everything that happens, keep before your eyes those to whom the same things happened, and how they were vexed, and treated them as strange things, and found fault with them; and now where are they? Nowhere. Why then do you, too, choose to act in the same way?"*
>
> -Marcus Aurelius-
> *Meditations 7.58*

Emotional vigilance is the last leg of the tripod. It's such a crucial function to the proper balance of our well-being. That's because it's the most human part of the tripod, therefore it should be of the utmost importance to maintain because emotions can get the absolute best of us, and push us into acting in a manner that we would not normally act. And actions driven by emotion are never thought out properly and almost always dangerous; dangerous to us and dangerous to others. Epictetus had the insight when he said:

> *"It shows a lack of refinement to spend a lot of time exercising, eating, drinking, defecating, or copulating. Tending to the body's needs should be done incidentally, as it were; the mind and its functions require the bulk of our attention."*

Emotional vigilance is the ability to recognize and sense when one's emotional state is on the precipice of affecting their actions. For example, when dealing with difficult people, it's the ability to sense when your anger and frustration is starting to go beyond your control to the point that you may say or do something that you will regret. And once you can recognize that emotions are taking over, you can then implement the tools within them to correct your behavior and maintain effective composure.

Without emotional vigilance, one can succumb to the negative effects that come from negative emotions. Having the keen ability to recognize when your emotions are reaching dangerous levels affords you the opportunity to get them in check on the spot before you lose control of them. This is where philosophy comes in. If studying history enriches our mental vigilance, then studying philosophy enriches our emotional vigilance because it brings clarity to the mind and offers the strength to endure.

> *"The closer a man comes to a clear mind, the closer he is to strength."*
>
> –Marcus Aurelius-

So, first things first, be a student of philosophy. You must keep in mind that merely reading a book on a certain philosophy once is not being a student. Being a student implies that you constantly train or learn from the lessons being taught, along with implementing and putting the wisdom into action. Seneca wrote a lot, often lengthy passages on what it is to be a student of philosophy and what one can gain from it. One passage, in particular, was simplified as such:

> "For nature does not give a man virtue, the process of becoming a good man is an art…but virtue only comes to a character which has been thoroughly schooled and trained and brought to a pitch of perfection by unremitting practice. We are born for it, but not with it."

Meaning, that virtue is not something we are born with. It is something that we learn as our time goes on, but also something that we should pay close attention to, study, and practice what it is to be virtuous. Wisdom, like any other perishable skill, can escape us if we neglect to practice it. Just like when it comes to tactics, when stress overwhelms us, we will default to our training, so you must train optimally. Philosophy is the same way when emotions begin to overwhelm you, you will recognize the issues and default to the virtues you have studied.

Besides the promise of gaining virtue through its study, philosophy allows us to examine how others of have handled similar situations. The passage from Marcus Aurelius that I opened this chapter with explains it well. There is no problem or obstacle you are experiencing now that someone, somewhere in history hasn't already confronted themselves. Examine how they reacted to it. If they chose to allow their emotions to get the best of them and they reacted negatively to it, how did that reaction work out for them in the end? If they took control over their emotions and endured it calmly, also examine how it worked out for them. Which person do you think persevered and came out the other side emotionally unscathed? The answer should be obvious.

Believe me when I tell you that I know just as well as any other cop reading this that dealing with verbally combative, difficult people is probably worse than physically combative people. Physical fights, more times than not, are very quick and swift. Maybe you get a scrape or two, but then you move on and tell your war story for times to come.

But I don't think anyone can deny that when a suspect is sitting in the back of your patrol vehicle yelling, screaming, and saying the most disrespectful things to try and get under your skin, while you're trying to type up arrest affidavits is by far more aggravating and stressful than a physical fight. The mental struggle always seems to supersede a physical one. It is during situations like that where emotional vigilance is of paramount importance to shield yourself from reacting in a primitive, impulsive manner.

Finding the moral means within you to combat challenging people is what sets you above the less moral. It's what showcases your true strength over theirs, not giving into the bait or falling into the trap of talking shit back to those who talk shit to you.

I remember one time while I was working on a specialized task force that targeted violent criminals, the team had arrested a group of juveniles for a multitude of violent felony charges. I was the lucky one who had the unforeseen opportunity to essentially have the ringleader detained in the back of my patrol cruiser.

As he sat in the back of my patrol cruiser, he proceeded to be verbally abusive towards me to include him saying he wanted to rape and kill my grandmother, all the while I was trying to complete paperwork. Of course, deep down inside, the emotional reaction made me want to reciprocate; to say some of the vilest things I could think of back, as well as wring his neck.

He was really starting to get under my skin. I could feel myself starting to fall prey to his trap. He wanted to get a reaction out of me. He wanted to drag me down to the depths where he was emotionally, as to feed his ego and gain a mental edge over me.

But because I am a practicing student of stoicism, I defaulted to the wisdom I had been studying. I was vigilant enough to recognize where my emotions were heading, came to a point of mental clarity, and immediately thought of a lecture from Epictetus from the *Enchiridion* that says when challenged, remember the tools I have within me to combat the challenge. In this case, it was patience. I realized that he was just a kid, he had not mattered or influenced my life prior to this encounter, he wouldn't matter or affect my life after, and I wouldn't allow him to influence it now.

I also thought of the reasons he was probably acting out: fear, embarrassment, shame, etc. He may have put up a tough front, but the way he was acting and talking towards me was nothing more than a result of his own shame and fear. He was acting out of natural fight or flight instinct and I could not fault him for that.

So, I no longer took any offense to his actions and found the patience inside me to completely and utterly ignore him as he went on a fifteen-minute tirade about raping and killing my family, letting him stew in his own negative influence instead of allowing it to consume me as well.

It eventually got to the point where he stopped and straight-up asked me if he had pissed me off at all. When I told him that he hadn't, he was shocked. And then to my surprise he actually apologized for everything he said about my family, and I didn't hear another word from him after that.

The unforeseen opportunity of having that young man in the back of my patrol cruiser had revealed why it was an opportunity. It was an opportunity because I was able to put the philosophy into action and prove to myself, and now to others, that the philosophy works if you accept it.

I could have gotten angry like I felt myself getting, I could have reciprocated the shit-talking like most other cops do, but chose not to. Because as Seneca had said:

"The greatest remedy for anger is delay."

The best way to correct your emotions and compose yourself is to stop for a few seconds before you react, analyze and dissect what it really is that is going on outside of your control, and finally to change your opinion of the situation in a way that it no longer angers or upsets you.

So, I leave you with this, if you're not embracing some sort of philosophy that has a virtuous aim, you are really doing yourself a great disservice. This job will eat you alive if you do not search for some sort of wisdom or virtue that will help you keep your emotions in check.

Afterthoughts

Remaining vigilant in all areas of your well-being is paramount for ensuring survival in law enforcement; physical survival as well as mental/emotional survival. Each aspect of vigilance is dependent on the other to thrive. If mental and physical vigilance make up the components of a train, then emotional vigilance is the track it needs to move on. Just like the tracks dictate where the train goes emotions can dictate our mental and physical states of well-being. If you don't train yourself physically and eat garbage, although it may stimulate you emotionally for a brief moment, it will affect your mental/emotional state in the long run with feelings of guilt or shame. Just like if you can't get your emotions in check and run yourself into depression, you won't have the drive or energy to train physically, and your emotions may even negatively affect you physically. The whole virtue of staying vigilant then collapses in on itself.

Seneca, who suffered throughout his life with intense asthma and other bouts of sickness, recognized the connection between the physical body and the mind, realizing that they affected each other, when he wrote in regards to recovering from a bout of sickness:

> *"Comforting thoughts contribute to a person's cure; anything that raises his spirits benefits him physically as well. It was my Stoic studies that saved me really."*

This is why it is so important to make sure you are staying vigilant with every aspect of your well-being.

If you haven't picked up on it yet while reading this book, each virtue builds upon each other. I first discussed the importance of humility and how you must properly balance a level of detachment with empathy when interacting with any demographic of society, which then flowed into the discussion of the need to balance humility out with vigilance that you do not leave yourself too unguarded when interacting with potentially dangerous individuals. But vigilance needs to be balanced out as well in order to prevent hypervigilance; a symptom of post-traumatic stress disorder (PTSD).

PART III

TRANQUILITY

"It is in your power to live free from compulsion and in the greatest tranquility of mind, even if all the world cries out against you as much as they choose."

-Marcus Aurelius-
Meditations 7.68

Vigilance is a great virtue to have, that's why I've made it a point to talk about it in this book, but if left unchecked vigilance can begin to blur and morph into hypervigilance. According to Dr. Kevin Gilmartin, a law enforcement psychologist with over twenty years of law enforcement service as well, described in his book *Emotional Survival for Law Enforcement*, the effects of what he coined the *emotional rollercoaster*. The emotional rollercoaster is the cycle of extreme emotional highs followed by extreme emotional lows.

As police officers, as well as military and other first responders, we go to work and experience some extreme scenarios that get our adrenaline and blood pressure going at full throttle, and in reality, for short periods of time. We drive fast, we get in foot chases, we get into physical fights, we have deadly weapons brandished on us, which forces us to have to use weapons on others, we see death accompanied with gore, and we see children, the elderly and mentally handicapped abused and taken advantage of in ways that are unfathomable to the average naïve citizen.

And as soon as that is all over, we are expected to cool the engines down and go about our business to the next call or incident, as if the last one didn't happen. And if you're a cop in an agency with a high call volume and high crime statistics, you ride the rollercoaster with exponentially greater frequencies of highs and lows.

And to add to the stress that we experience from the calls we ride, we also have to deal with how command staff, men and women who haven't been on a call in a very long time and are more or less very detached to the changing of times, will analyze and interpret our actions if they come under review. And god forbid you made any type of honest mistake or lapse in judgment, we also have to deal with the negative feedback we'll receive from some of the more egotistical officers in our agency.

Because let's face it, law enforcement is like high school all over again; everyone knows everyone's business, good and bad, but they only concentrate on the bad. And you know you'll hear all about yourself in the rumor mill.

Long term hypervigilance can create mental and emotional turmoil, causing PTSD, anxiety, fear, and paranoia. And that is why we cannot allow hypervigilance to be a long term problem. In order to balance out vigilance and deter hypervigilance, we have to find tranquility in our lives.

To explain better, vigilance is the part of us that enables us to detect unforeseen, yet inevitable, stress-inducing problems and allows us to start devising a plan to combat it. Tranquility is the other part of us that helps us to take that problem, the one that is masked in all its unnecessary stress and evil, and allows us to dissect and unmask it all the way down to its roots. Once stripped down, you then can see the problem for what it really is, something that is solvable, endurable, bearable, or in all reality, not as big of a deal that you made it out to be.

It is at that point you can begin to control your opinion of the problem and bring upon yourself tranquility; a state of internal calmness despite the perceived chaos around you, and allow the stress of the issue to flow right through you without even leaving a mark; the root of what stoicism is. Marcus had a good method for the dissection of internal anguish in order to change the perception of it:

> "Take away your opinion, and then there is taken away the complaint 'I have been harmed'. Take away the complaint, 'I have been harmed', and the harm is taken away."

Your problem is only as bad as your opinion perceives it to be. And with a tranquil mind, any problem can be seen for what it truly is, and they're never as horrible and ugly as you make them out to be. As Epictetus said:

> "In general, remember it is we who torment, it is we who makes difficulties for ourselves—that is, our opinions do."

Think of tranquility as a possible fourth leg to vigilance; vigilance of the spirit.

> "Catastrophes are circumstances of our existence which we cannot change. What we can do is adopt a noble spirit, such a spirit as befits a good man, so that we may bear up bravely under all that fortune sends us and bring our will into tune with nature's."
>
> –Seneca-

On Dealing With Facebook Lawyers

"When someone criticizes you or speaks badly of you, remember that they are doing what they believe is right. They cannot be guided by your views, only their own; so, if their views are wrong, they are the ones who suffer insofar as they are misguided. If someone declares a true proposition to be false, the proposition remains true, and they are the ones whose ignorance is exposed."

-Epictetus-
Enchiridion 42

All platforms of social media were born out of good intentions; the intention being to essentially bring people together from all walks of life. To inspire people, to incite positive conversations about political and social events, etc. But since its inception, social media has become a conduit for the spread of false information, knee-jerk reactions to events without having all the facts, incoherent rants that meander on with poor punctuation and without ever getting to a point, arguments instead of conversations, and the ultimate self-procured fallacy of viewing oneself as a Facebook lawyer.

These pseudo-intellectual types then like to regurgitate all their false information in any way they can, especially when it comes to interacting with law enforcement. The clearest indicator that you are about to interact with one of these "lawyers" is when they begin a simple, non-custodial, cordial conversation with: "Am I being detained?" Cue the eye roll.

I don't believe I need to preach to the choir when I begin to describe just how agitating these characters are. Time and time again, I've seen how easy it is for fellow officers, mostly younger ones and myself included in my rookie days, to fall into constitutional debates with the most uninformed people who try to tell them how to do their job; and I see how worked up they can get trying to prove that they are right.

There is absolutely no use in falling prey to it. Social media lawyers, as irritating as they can be, are almost always wrong in their assumptions. You know they're wrong, and you know you're right, so why go back and forth with them?

At the end of the day, they're the ones who have to suffer in life being ignorant of the Constitution of the land they live in, and you get peace of mind (tranquility) in being an informed individual. This is where tranquility shields you from the frustration of dealing with them.

As long as you know within your soul that you're acting lawfully, constitutionally, and you are procedurally accurate, then let them put on their show in telling you how you should be doing your job. Any push back by you is a trap. A trap to get an emotionally negative reaction out of you so that they can broadcast it to their alma mater, social media.

That's not to say that you should ignore them outright. If you are tranquil enough to have your emotions in check and you utilize humility, then you may want to try educating the individual. Show them or explain where they are misunderstanding the way things are. If they are humble enough to receive your explanation openly, then you've won. If they're stubbornly closed-minded and refuse to accept their ignorance, then no worry, because you've still won by not falling into their trap of being aggressively confrontational. Always keep in mind:

> *"When someone caught in an argument hardens to stone, there is just no more reasoning with them."*
>
> –Epictetus-

Once someone refuses to listen to good advice or the acceptance of criticism, you're better off leaving them to their ignorance in order to save yourself the headache of trying to impose your side.

Now on the other hand, if one of these Facebook lawyers actually has a leg to stand on with their critique of your duties, you need to be humble and accept that you are wrong. Hardening to stone in your wrong position will only stress you out, make you look like you do not know what you're doing, and potentially cause you embarrassment if it ends up online. Epictetus tells us :

"If any man is able to convince me and show me that I do not think or act right, I will gladly change; for I seek the truth by which no man was ever injured. But he is injured who abides by his error and ignorance."

This is where some things swing back full circle to humility; always bear in mind that just because you are a cop, it does not mean you are always going to be right, otherwise you will drive yourself crazy trying to be right; the opposite of tranquility.

You are still human and capable of being uninformed on certain matters. If you put your reasoning in practice, you'll realize that you can't know everything. For example, take out your state's respective law book. Look at it in all its 5-inch thick, and several thousand-page glory. Ask yourself, do you absolutely know every single thing that's in it? All the criminal law, traffic law, civil law, administrative law, or procedural law? Of course not, because there are so many aspects of the law book that don't specifically apply to the enforcement side.

Now, take it a step further and concentrate on just the traffic and criminal law sections of the book. Do you honestly know every single one of those laws? I doubt it. It's good to try, but there is just too much to remember, which is why every agency has specialized units that deal with enforcing specific areas of criminal and traffic law.

So, if someone, especially a Facebook lawyer citizen, exposes a small hole in your knowledge of something specific, take it as an opportunity to grow both intellectually as well as characteristically. Calmly take the time to double-check your facts before refuting their argument. If you're mistaken, politely admit it and get yourself out of the hole before you make it any deeper.

In doing so, you free yourself from the stress of complete embarrassment, or worse, even the stress of a complaint because the citizen felt it necessary to inform your chain of command just how inept you were.

And if they really did have a leg to stand on, and can prove that you didn't know what you were doing, well now you have to explain to your supervisor why you weren't doing your job correctly. Again, added stress you don't want if you had just admitted your mistake in the first place.

On Navigating Department Politics

"No longer let any other man hear you find fault with the court of life."

-Marcus Aurelius-
Meditations 8.9

A lot of the times in law enforcement today, it always seems that our greatest enemy is not the gang member with the gun in his waistband, but our own agencies. We second guess decisions because we fear administrative sanctions, we hesitate to act because we fear our actions being investigated, we don't take control of situations out of fear of getting a rudeness complaint which will then lead into, you guessed it, an internal investigation.

You may think that this topic is going to be a long-winded but it won't because the answer is simple: never hesitate to act because in the heat of the moment it is your ass and your partner's ass on the line. So, act first, worry about scrutiny later. As long as you can go home at the end of the day, look in the mirror and know that you acted morally, ethically, lawfully, and didn't blatantly disregard policy or direct orders, then you should be morally content with your response.

To shed some perspective on the career, when you take the time to think about it, you'll come to understand that at the end of the day, this is still just a job. Now, I don't say that to downplay the level of effort you put forth or make an excuse not to conduct yourself to the highest ethical level possible in the profession, but to make you realize that it is, in fact, just a job. And to put some more perspective on it, every job has the same exact problems that you feel are exclusive to police.

You can choose to leave law enforcement and go into the corporate world, and you'll still find micro-managing bosses, paperwork that has deadlines, strictly timed meetings at the most inconvenient times (in our case, court), long commutes, stressful days, unhappy customers, etc. The only difference is the degree of the potential exposure to danger and horrific human conditions.

Now, in keeping with the stoic mindset, the only way to navigate the problems and politics of your department is first, not to allow it to affect you negatively and second, not to begrudgingly vocalize your contempt about your own perceived horrible working conditions (if you want a poor reputation, that is the fast track way of getting there), and third, realize that you will make mistakes.

As para-militaristic as law enforcement is, with the high level of expectations, you are still not immune to making mistakes. The quicker you realize that you will make a mistake, and you will, a lot of them, the quicker you can find to peace with the long career ahead.

If you know that you did make a mistake out of ignorance or a slight lapse in judgment, then take ownership of it, don't make excuses, accept your punishment and learn from it.

You also have to understand that the command staff, who may be a little out of the loop on how the streets are nowadays, have a job to do just like you do; and that is merely to keep things in running order, to build and keep the public trust between the agency and citizens, and to hold officers responsible for mistakes in order to maintain a high standard agency-wide. They too have to answer to a higher power, whether it be a mayor, commissioner, or the biggest boss, the citizens of the community. And I'm saying this as someone who has never been in any sort of position to discipline a subordinate. I merely just understand their side of it.

None of it is personal, and if you take it personally, then it's because you have too big an ego to accept responsibility for your actions, and haven't found the tranquility to accept how the chain of command works.

This may be an unpopular opinion to some. Some may make excuses and say that "Lieutenant So-and-So is out to get me for no reason" or "Captain So-and-So just doesn't like me" or "The command staff is corrupt" etc. And maybe there is some truth to any of those excuses. So I would ask, why is the Lieutenant out to get you? Because there's always a reason.

What did you do in the past? And what measures did you take to rectify it?

Why does the captain not like you? Again, what have you done in the past? Did you rectify it? Are you a hard worker? Is the command staff really corrupt? Or do you just not agree with the policies and decisions they hand down that you must follow? Try checking your ego and stop being paranoid. Realize that there's a bigger picture to every decision that's made than just to mess with you specifically. Once you can realize that, you will find tranquility.

Remember, you cannot control what happens in the politics of the department. You can only control your reaction to it. So, if a policy comes out that you don't agree with, don't complain about it and fight it tooth and nail. Read it and understand it. Does it violate constitutional rights (unlikely, but there are always exceptions to the rule)? Sure, then, by all means, push back. But does it appear to have a good reason behind it, whether you agree or not? Then you must embrace it, and fall in line.

When you fall in line, do your job, and work hard, no supervisor in their right mind is going to mess with you. If you're a hard worker and make a minor mistake here and there, which you will, no supervisor is going to purposely hang you out to do dry, so relax. Again, at the end of the day, this is just a job that you can exchange for another one.

On Surviving Police High School

"Failure to observe what is in the mind of another has seldom made a man unhappy; but those who do not observe the movements of their own minds must of necessity be unhappy."

-Marcus Aurelius-
Meditations 2.8

When you left high school, you probably thought you would never have to deal with rumors, deceit, backstabbing, or cliques. That is until you entered into law enforcement. The rumors, deceit, and backstabbing may even be worse than you remembered it. Now today there are websites like LEOAffairs.com that perpetuate the slander because so many "brave" cops can go on there under a pseudonym or anonymous profile and spread their hate about their agency and coworkers. God forbid you make any type of rookie mistake, or even a common mistake, you can rest assured that you'll be talked about.

Again, this section won't be long either because the childish nature in which some officers conduct themselves towards other officers is not worth giving them the reaction they so desire. Those officers are so miserable and so unaware of themselves and their weaknesses, that they feel the need to project their misery on others whenever someone else makes a mistake.

So, to be brief, in order to achieve to a tranquil mind about being the hot topic in an agency discussion is to remember two things:

1. You are going to make mistakes—law enforcement is a long career, thirty years in some agencies, and the possibility of surviving it mistake-less is impossible. So, make your mistakes, learn from them, and grow. And whoever feels the need to say something negative about your character afterward will be in your shoes sooner than later. Just make sure to be the bigger person and don't stoop to their level by belittling them. They'll feel stupid in front of you even if you don't address it with them.
2. You can do everything right, and still someone will find a reason to slander you. It's that old adage, "you can do 99 things correctly, but that 100th thing you do wrong is all that people will remember." Again, this is a long career and no matter how morally and ethically

you conduct yourself, someone is still not going to like you, and it's usually the insecure, miserable people who won't. In that case, take it as an opportunity to show them some humility and help them in altering their demeanors. If they stay stuck in their misery, then so be it. Move on and choose to not allow them to affect you.

Lastly, as Marcus Aurelius said, worrying about what others are doing and thinking does nothing for you except inflame your insecurities. Concentrating on yourself with the intention of improving your own character is how to navigate around the negativity of the rumor mill into a state of tranquility.

On Being Continually Pissed Off

"Consider that men will do the same things even though you would burst with rage."

-Marcus Aurelius-
Meditations 8.4

I'll begin by saying this, if you have failed in your emotional vigilance, you are probably the archetypical officer who is constantly pissed off at the world, miserable, and unapproachable; and I would know because I was that officer. Angry for a laundry list of reasons: high crime agency and low pay, getting passed over for positions I thought I deserved or was more qualified for, other lazy and inept officers, poor command staff and leadership, difficult citizens who end up complaining, Facebook lawyers, constant court subpoenas even when I wasn't needed (especially when they were the first thing in the morning after a midnight shift), and the list goes on.

The Stoic Cop: Policing Through Stoic Virtue

All that pent-up stress and anger stuffed inside becomes a ticking time bomb that is triggered by the most minuscule set back in life and we end up taking it out on our coworkers, spouses, family, and friends. We walk around with a tattoo on our foreheads that explicitly advertises "fuck off," complain how everything is bullshit, and are skeptical of everyone's intentions.

And then it begins to go downhill from there. In order to decompress, we openly complain about tasks and people to a roll call room full of other officers and ultimately create a reputation for ourselves as being unapproachable, negative, not a team player, etc. And then once that reputation begins to grow, good luck trying to get any of those specialty spots you put in for because you most likely will not get them, which keeps the train you're now riding continuing full steam ahead.

My wife used to work at a bar that utilized off duty officers from the department I was working for at the time. That agency was relatively large and it was difficult to know every single officer who worked there, so needless to say I didn't really have any personal connection to most officers within the agency. My wife would come home and tell me how a lot of good officers worked off-duty at that bar and how she got along with them great, and she always made sure to tell them that I worked for the agency as well, because we all know how cops are.

To make a long story short, one particular night there was an officer who worked off duty whom I didn't know nor had I ever even heard of, and of course, my wife made sure to tell him that I worked for the agency as well. At some point in the night, my wife was taking her dinner break when this particular officer approached her and asked her to share some of her dinner. She respectfully declined at which time this particular "officer" called her a "*cunt.*" And then after some back and forth dialogue, he proceeded to tell her that he was going to "*shove his cock in her mouth.*"

Of course, when I found out about it, I wanted to punish him myself, having no idea who he even was, all I knew was he was a real piece of shit. I decided to take the high ground and made a complaint against him.

What I had found out about him, later on, was that he was "connected" somewhere in the agency. He was on a specialized unit and was almost invincible in the agency. Now, the complaint did get investigated and was ultimately sustained, but nothing ever really happened to him. This "officer" had disrespected my wife, disrespected me, and disrespected the badge, but still, he was a golden boy so he got to keep his spot on specialized units and was even allowed to put in for other ones.

I harbored a lot of hatred and anger towards how it was handled. I was angry with the despicable excuse for an "officer" and I was angry with the agency for holding no accountability.

I carried that baggage with me pretty much everywhere. I wore my frustration on my face a lot of the time and verbalized my thoughts about the agency constantly. And then it all came to a head during the selection process for a particular specialized unit. Ten people had put in for it, including myself and that officer. Needless to say, I went into that interview pissed off that he was even allowed to apply.

I had also found out prior that one of the sergeants on the unit that I was applying for was also that officer's sergeant in the last specialized unit they worked together, so I was heated even more. I had pre-planned in my head that I was going to express to the interview panel just how I really felt about it if asked.

Fast forward to the interview. I thought the majority of the interview went very well. I was confident, answered all the questions honestly and thoroughly, etc. I definitely felt that I had the potential to be a good candidate, not necessarily the chosen one, but definitely in the running for it; until the last question. They asked me: if there was one thing that I could change about the agency, what would it be and why?

Needless to say, I told them how I really felt. I recounted the story of that particular officer and respectfully trashed the agency for holding no one accountable for his egregious conduct. I then gave the panel (which consisted of two sergeants, one of which was that sergeant who I mentioned before, and a captain) an ultimatum. I told them that I absolutely refused to work with that officer if it was decided that multiple people were going to get chosen and we happened to be the choices. It was either going to be him or me.

After I had spilled my disdain for the agency and that officer, I could see it in their faces that *it just wasn't going to work out in the end.* They told me that they appreciated my raw honesty and thanked me for my time. In the end, I did not get the position, and that particular officer was one of two or three chosen for the spot.

And of course, this drove more anger and disgust into my core. I had allowed my anger to sabotage me because I could not let it go. I could not stifle my frustration for a few minutes while I interviewed for a spot that I wanted. That officer won again and this time it was all my own fault.

Had I been wiser, I would have just filed the complaint as I did originally and let the process take its course as it did and been satisfied with that. Although the results weren't ideal, people like that officer will eventually be seen for who they really are and that would have been enough to achieve tranquility on the matter. But instead, I was in a hole so deep of frustration that it would have been almost impossible to get out, and probably would have taken a few years of reconciliation in my attitude to fix. Reputations don't die easy, they die hard.

If you find yourself in the same situation, realize that it's fixable, and you can redeem yourself from it, but it will definitely be an uphill battle that will take some time. So, the first step in the process of overcoming your anger is finding the tranquility to succeed with your emotional vigilance. I will circle back to Seneca from earlier: "The best remedy for anger is delay."

When you feel yourself getting angry at some aspect of this job, whether it be with an antagonistic citizen or a micromanaging supervisor, before you begin to verbalize or act out, you need to stop and consider this:

> "If it is not right, do not do it. If it is not true, do not say it. For let your impulse be within your own power."
> –Marcus Aurelius-

Once you've kept yourself from acting out irrationally, analyze what it is that you're angry at: did a citizen call you a "pig" and tell you how to do your job? Or perhaps a supervisor disapproved of a report that you thought you wrote well? In other words, trivial circumstances that occur regularly, that have happened to you before, and will more than likely happen again at some point if not that very same day.

Think of how you handled it before, or how another officer handled it and didn't think anything of the circumstance other than to just fix or rectify it. So, why are you about to lose your mind over it now? When you put the situation into a perspective like that, only then will you find how ridiculous it would be to get mad at that point, and you will hopefully default back to a state of tranquility. The next step is to let it go and not dwell on it.

> *"Think of your last hour. Let the wrong that is done by a man stay where the wrong was done."*
> –Marcus Aurelius- Meditations 7.29

Leave the baggage right there where it is. Carrying it around with you will keep you from tranquility; just like the physical act of actually carrying around heavy baggage, it will fatigue and exhaust you. And once someone reaches a state of pure exhaustion, the weight needs to be unloaded safely or you might unload it where you shouldn't. This means the emotional baggage will either lead you to one big explosive incident of rage in order to relieve yourself quickly or turn you into the dreaded complainer that no one likes to be around because it gradually relieves the baggage. Don't allow yourself to be either of these two. Leave wrong where the wrong was done. Let it go and continue in your state of tranquility.

If you can master this analysis of what you are about to do out of anger, you have achieved tranquility. If you haven't achieved tranquility there and then, the process shall continue on. Analyze what it is you're getting angry at. Did your favorite coffee spot run out of your favorite flavor? Ok, well think of all the other people who share your same flavor and aren't getting it either. Do you think that they are punching their steering wheels? And if they are, don't you see how stupid they would look if you saw them getting made over a coffee order?

Being pissed off all the time is too much work, it's fatiguing, and it's not worth it to harbor it. You will only sever relationships and create an image of you in other officers minds who haven't even met or worked with you before; your reputation will proceed you.

As you've probably picked up by now, I've worked for multiple agencies, currently on my third one. There were a multitude of reasons as to why I left my second one, but one in particular is that I was disgruntled and carrying around the baggage and disdain everywhere I went. And because of that, as I said before, I never got any positions I put in for within the agency. My ego got too big, and I began to blame a lot of factors for why I wasn't getting picked for anything, such as: I was good at patrol and they wanted to keep me there, the person who was choosen over me had an "in," the selection process was already predetermined, etc.; I took it all personally like it was an attack on my skillset and character as the reason why I was not getting picked. I never took into account that it was probably my attitude, my bad reputation, which proceeded me or that I just wasn't prepared enough despite the fact that I thought I was. And so, essentially, you could say that I ran away to another agency.

When I got to my current agency, I took it upon myself to make a fresh start. I tried being more positive and receptive to criticism. I don't take things overly personally (although I have my moments, we all do) and I humbled myself a little. I don't wear my negative emotions on my face, and I try not to judge other officers.

With just those slight changes of attitude, a lot of opportunities have come my way. I got into a specialized unit almost as soon as my probation was up and am currently doing the fast-paced type of policing I got into policing for.

So, practice delaying your anger and give yourself time to analyze what is triggering you, dissect it, and you'll see how ridiculous it is to get angry. You'll begin to recognize your attitude and how it's being perceived by others. Only then will you have the clear head not to take things so personally and see the opportunities that begin to open up for you.

On Death

"Since it is possible that you may depart from life this very moment, regulate every act and thought accordingly."
-Marcus Aurelius-
Meditations 2.11

Memento Mori (remember you must die); probably the most notably well-recognized Latin phrase associated with the Stoics, even recognized by people who don't attribute it to stoicism. Why is it so notable? Because it's a delicate reminder to all on the outcome of our existence.

According to DailyStoic.com, *Memento Mori* is believed to have originated from an ancient Roman tradition where an Emperor, after having achieved great victory in a military campaign would be paraded around the streets of Rome, and during the parade, the Emperor would be idolized and viewed as a god by all Romans alike.

So, in order to keep life in perspective, to keep him aware and humble of his inevitable demise, there would be a slave in the chariot with him, standing right behind the Emperor, who would whisper to him: *"Respice post te. Hominem te esse memento. Memento Mori."* Meaning: Look behind. Remember you are mortal. Remember you must die."

Over the course of human history many cultures have practiced the art of reminding themselves that death is real, unavoidable, and something we all have in common. Some cultures hold festivals to remember the dead and bring a reminder to a predetermined future. Some cultural revolutions like the Renaissance have produced pieces of artwork that have stood the test of time and depicted stark reminders of mortality. Other cultures have practiced the act of carrying around with them pieces of jewelry that give them a constant reminder of their fate.

The ancient Stoics, specifically Marcus Aurelius, Epictetus, and Seneca have all meditated on their mortalities, and for good reason, because it reminds them how they should live their lives with whatever indeterminate amount of time they have left. Seneca posed an important question in one of his letters:

"You want to live, but do you know how to live?"

That brings us back to Marcus Aurelius's meditation mentioned at the beginning of this section and gives us insight as to why it is important to meditate on mortality. If you remind yourself of your inevitable death, it should help you determine how you should be acting, or better yet, living in that moment. Are you wasting your life or making the best of it? Are you making righteous decisions to better yourself and enrich the lives of others around you, or are your decisions making a mess of your life and the lives of others? Are you making things right with people whom you had a falling out, or are you holding a meaningless grudge you've been carrying for a year?

The thought of death and its shadow that constantly follows you around should drive you to make those decisions in life that you may have been putting off. It should drive you to make amends, conquer a goal, leave a lasting impression in someone else's life, etc. But it's not like that anymore. In modern society, we avoid the thought and topic of death at all costs.

Modern decorum is all about "Live, laugh, love" and other quotes of that magnitude, which have their purpose in the how to live life, but they don't prepare one mentally for when life does end.

Death and law enforcement are not mutually exclusive. It is a very real possibility that you may go to work and you may die that day. And as much as people say they understand that they are signing up for a job that may kill them, or that they may have to kill someone else, I believe that they only understand on the surface, but they don't truly understand the absolute reality of it. I say that because when I look back at when I decided to become a cop, I understood the potential consequences of the profession, but didn't really give too much thought to the realm of possibility that it would happen to me. And I also don't believe that I'm the only one.

Think about it. The phrase in which we've discussed in vigilance, "complacency kills" only exists because officers get complacent. And why do they get complacent, besides the obvious answer *laziness*? Because they either never really understood the reality of death, or because they've forgotten the delicacy of their mortality.

Another example is dealing with officers we know who are killed in the line of duty, and how hard it hits an entire agency. One reason, in my opinion, it hurts fellow officers so much more than it should is because, again, the shadow of death that lurks behind us all gets overlooked.

We place an overabundance of value on the lives of ourselves and lives of our brothers and sisters but never check it with the reminder that we all will perish at some point, and that is why death is scary and death is something we ignore and avoid, and which is why when it does sneak up and happen, our whole world comes crashing in on us. The opposite of what it is to achieve tranquility.

I remember the first time I realized the lethality of this job. I had heard my best friend on the shift I was working on at the time come over the radio and say that he was behind a stolen vehicle that was beginning to drive recklessly. The vehicle didn't flee all that far until it crashed and the driver exited the vehicle. The radio traffic after that was, at that point my career, the most heart-stopping yet adrenaline-pumping traffic I had ever heard. It was a mixture of inaudible, high pitched yelling with the chaos going in the background. Deciphered somewhere in that horrific radio traffic, I heard "shots fired."

I had already been lights and sirens to him before that radio traffic aired, so I was close. As I got on scene, I could smell the fresh expulsion of gunfire like you would on the range, except this wasn't the range, this was real life. This wasn't training, or a live drill, or practice, or scenarios, or whatever controlled environment you want to call it. This was absolutely real life.

The suspect had gotten out of the stolen vehicle after it crashed and began shooting at my friend. Thankfully, that friend and officer wasn't injured and the suspect was apprehended, but the job got real for me at that point. Since then, I have been on the scene of a plethora of officer-involved shootings, some with officer injuries, but thankfully none with officer deaths.

But even though I say "thankfully" I still keep it in my mind that there is still a possibility for death to occur. I do not want to be caught off guard by it.

So, how do we go about coming to terms with death? If you ask any of the ancient Stoics, they would probably answer by saying something along the lines that "the terms of death were set at the time of your birth and you should have already accepted it." But for those who have a hard time with it, let's come to terms now.

In the *Enchiridion*, Epictetus describes mortality and the terms of it as such:

> *"Consider when, on a voyage, your ship is anchored; if you go on shore to get water you may along the way amuse yourself with picking up shellfish, or an onion. However, your thoughts and continual attention ought to be bent towards the ship, waiting for the captain to call on board; you must then immediately leave all these things, otherwise you will be thrown in the ship bound neck and feet like a sheep.*
>
> *So it is with life. If instead of an onion or a shellfish, you are given a wife or child, which is fine. But if the captain calls you must run to the ship, leaving them and regarding none of them."*

A ship anchored in the harbor is temporary, much like our lives are, and the captain commanding the ship is nature or whatever god you believe in. Going to shore and enjoying what's there is essentially our lives. But we must be ready to leave the shore and all of our attachments to it behind once the captain calls for us to go.

This passage also is very relatable to law enforcement, especially the part about having a family but being ready to leave them at any moment. Think of when you're getting ready to go to work and just before you leave your house to go, you say goodbye to your significant other and kids if you have them. You then get into your vehicle and go to work. Now, do you honestly put that moment into your realization that it may very well be the last time that you see your family? What was the tone when you said goodbye? Did you even say goodbye?

When I married my wife, I put it in my vows that I would always promise to say goodbye before I leave for work for that very reason that it could possibly be the last time. Now, have I always upheld that vow? Regrettably, no, because I am human. But I keep my mortality at the forefront of my mind so that I always remember to at least make the attempt, even if we are fighting, because death is very real.

And not only is our death very real, but the death of our fellow officers is very real, which is why you must remember that everyone is mortal. If we have our understanding of mortality in check, we will be able to grieve graciously and not be completely devastated by it. As Seneca said in a letter in regards to the death of a friend:

> "When one has lost a friend, one's eyes should be neither dry nor streaming. Tears, yes, there should be, but not lamentation…Would you like to know what lies behind

extravagant weeping and wailing? In our tears we are trying to find the means of proving that we feel the loss. We are not governed by our grief, but parading it."

Meaning, that if we have prepared our minds for the possibility of our close friends dying, then we shouldn't be extravagantly crying because then it just becomes an act; unless one hasn't properly prepared themselves for death, then extravagant crying proves their lack of understanding of mortality.

It's absolutely ok to grieve, and everyone grieves differently, but stoics will prepare themselves beforehand for the grief and will not make an act out of it in front of others to show that they are grieving harder than anyone else is. I think it would be safe to say that we've all encountered someone who has acted that exact way. Don't you think it to be foolish?

To reiterate, you must meditate on mortality. You must always bear in mind that someone, yourself included, may be here one minute and gone the next. You will find the tranquility you seek about death and no longer fear it, but embrace it honorably.

Hell Ain't A Bad Place To Be

"Sometimes even to live be an act of courage."

-Seneca-
Letters from a Stoic LXXVIII

During my current tenure as a police officer, I have encountered the unfortunate circumstance of suicide; both directly and indirectly. Directly knowing officers who have killed themselves, and indirectly knowing them; nevertheless, it always makes you wonder what could have been so bad. You see these same individuals one day, normal in demeanor, no warning signs, and the next day you hear of their demise. Of course, I began this book describing my bout with hell, but it still doesn't satiate the curiosity as to why or what brings a person to that decision. There are just too many variables and every person is wired differently. Even I didn't recognize why I was in my own personal hell until after I came out the other side unscathed.

The main variable that I later recognized to be a factor in my bout was the night shift paradigm. In a medical article called *Night Work and the Risk of Depression,* Dr. Peter Angerer and his team researched multiple decades worth of medical studies linking night shift work and depression.

They concluded there is no question that the night shift interferes with the body's natural circadian chrono-biological rhythm along with impeding hormone balances, reducing the production of melatonin, and increasing the level of carcinogens in the body. And although there is evidence to support the link between night shift work and depression, based on four to ten year-long observations of groups of workers, the evidence is still pretty weak in terms of consistent results to be absolutely conclusive.

However, in another article titled: *Low Vitamin D Status and Suicide: A Case-Control Study of Active Duty Military Service Members,* the study of active duty military members and vitamin D deficiencies concluded that some of the lowest shown levels of vitamin D in the body yielded an increased risk of suicide. This is because more advanced evidence has supported that vitamin D influences functions in the brain of up to 1,000 genes that potentially contribute to neurotrophic and neuroprotective effects, all of which could influence suicidal behavior. As we all know, some of the best sources of vitamin D come directly from sunlight; and what don't we get enough of, if any, on night shift? Sunlight.

This definitely gives a little more insight into my own situation. I do have to admit that when I found these results, I laughed. During my darkest hours, my mother had picked up on my change in behavior. I had told her that I was unhappy with the constant darkness experienced during the winter months on night shift, although I never really admitted to her my true feelings, and she suggested that I take some over-the-counter vitamin D supplements. Of course, I didn't at first because I'm stubborn like that, but after I snapped out of it and began reading *Meditations,* I also tried taking some vitamin D supplements.

I can't say that it made a noticeable difference, but after reading the conclusion in the study of military personnel, there may be something to it. Not to mention that I had forced myself to start waking up before noon in order to help myself get adequate amounts of sunlight. Needless to say, I am still here today.

Suicide is all too prevalent in this profession and seems to be increasing each year. According to Blue H.E.L.P, an organization that compiles statistics of law enforcement-related suicides has reported that since 2016 the number of reported law enforcement-related suicides has increased every year. In 2016 there were 143 suicides, 2017; 172, 2018; 174, and 2019; 228.

Blue H.E.L.P does offer the disclaimer that their numbers only reflect the number of reported law enforcement-related suicides and does not reflect the actual number that may include unreported ones being classified as law enforcement-related. Although with that disclaimer, it doesn't prove that police suicides as a whole are increasing, but it still brings into question as to why the number of reported ones is increasing.

And with all the organizations and programs provided out there, such as Blue H.E.L.P, which also offers services to help first responders cope with their issues, why is the reported number increasing? I'm obviously not a licensed medical psychologist and cannot offer any medical remedies or answers, but what I do have is the philosophy that saved me, and this philosophy I can pass on.

Stoicism does require coming to terms with one's mortality, and how death is a natural discourse of life, not something to be feared because it is out of our control, but let us be clear right now; although death is absolutely natural and an honorable part of a long fulfilling life, suicide is within our controlled, reasoned choice and inherently unnatural. Suicidal thoughts may be more common today than in decades past, but there is a reason it is still taboo; because it is an unnatural act, it defies instincts. Never confuse the acceptance of a natural death with that of an unnatural act of suicide.

Seneca wrote a lot on suicide, more than I have come across from any other Stoic. From what I've gathered, due to his long bouts with illness, he seems to have contemplated it at times in life, but through his stoic virtue, came to the conclusion of having reasoned against it. Specifically, in letter LXX-

VIII he described a time that he was so sick that he wanted to cut his life short.

He claimed that although that he felt he was brave enough to face his death, he knew that his loving father, in old age, was not brave enough to accept his death, and reasoned with himself against his own suicide. Deciding then to endure his pain and being brave enough to live, he proclaimed that "sometimes even to live be an act of courage." And courage, as we know, is a valued virtue with the Stoics.

This part of his letter is important to point out. Seneca was on the verge of taking his own life from all the pain he had to endure; in his case it was physical, but we as cops know that a lot of our pain lurks deep within our mind that we choose to not show anyone.

But in the midst of Seneca's pain and suffering, and thoughts of suicide, he came to the realization that he had reasons to live, and that reason kept him from carrying out his plan. This is proof that we all have some reason to live. Even if you don't recognize it immediately, if you simply get out of your head and look around, you will be able to see those reasons.

Maybe it's your kids, your dogs or cats, your significant other, siblings, etc. Believe me, there is always a reason to live if you pause for a moment and look. In a later letter where he wrote about the nature of suicide again, he came to a firmer conclusion against it:

The Stoic Cop: Policing Through Stoic Virtue

"The good man should go on living as he ought to, not just as long as he likes. The man who does not value his wife or a friend highly enough to hold on a little longer in life, who persists in dying in spite of them, is a thoroughly self-indulgent character.

Seneca then continued on to describe his healing process. I know I mentioned this quote in another section in the book, but it came from this particular letter and is relevant to the story. He exclaimed that:

"Comforting thoughts contribute to a person's cure; anything that raises his spirits benefits him physically as well. It was my Stoic studies that saved me really."

This goes to show that until you can get over that confusing hurdle of recognizing your reasons to live, only then can you begin your healing process, and it all starts with your mindset; changing your perception of the problem and seeing the silver lining, resurging the will to fight, and ultimately mastering what Ryan Holiday calls *the art of acquiescence;* being able to accept bad circumstances without protest.

Seneca then ends the letter with the realization that "everything hangs on one's thinking…a man is unhappy because he has convinced himself that he is unhappy." All the stoics have said something along those lines because that is the foundation of stoicism; altering your perception of the hell you feel that you are in. Only you can create the hell that you see around you. Your opinions are your own worst enemy. This is why I believe in the lyric from the legendary band AC/DC: "Hell ain't a bad place to be."

I don't mean that in the sense that feeling suicidal isn't a bad thing to feel. I'm not saying that you need to change your perception on suicide being a bad thing into being a good thing. I mean only whatever circumstances or hell you find yourself in, that you feel are bad enough to lead you down that path, are not as bad as your opinions make them out to be as long as you find the will to view them as such.

If you tell yourself over and over again, making it a mantra that "hell ain't a bad place to be," then it will help you begin to have a different perspective on the issue plaguing you. Remember, mindset and perspective is all we have in our control, so with the right thinking and perspective you can pull yourself from the depths of that hell and hold on longer. It is possible to control your perceived chaos.

On Reflection

"Men seek retreats for themselves, houses in the country, seashores, and mountains; and you too, are wont to desire such things very much. But this is altogether a mark of the common sort of men. For it is in your power whenever you choose, to retire into yourself. For there is no retreat that is quieter or freer from trouble than a man's own soul, especially when he has within him such thoughts that by looking into them, he is immediately in perfect tranquility; and in tranquility there is nothing else than the good ordering the mind. Constantly then give to yourself this retreat, and renew yourself."

-Marcus Aurelius-
Meditations 4.3

Ask any seasoned or retired police officer for advice on surviving long term in this career and you'll hear more times than not to have a hobby or friends outside of law enforcement. And it's absolutely true. I for one, as I mentioned previously, love working out and I love doing yard work. Both help me empty my mind almost completely at times.

Other officers I know or have met drive motorcycles, work on cars, and believe it or not, participate in medieval live action role playing (LARPing). And although all of those are great hobbies that help clear the mind and de-stress someone, they don't necessarily solve the internal issues that cause the stress in the first place.

What Marcus points out in this passage, and Seneca has pointed out in some of his writings, is that doing something, in his example vacationing, isn't the answer to solving personal issues and achieving a long-term tranquil mind. They are short-term de-stressors.

If you think about it, when you travel and go on vacation, yes, you are stimulated and de-stressed by the novelty of the new scenery. But look at who you brought with you; yourself and all your personal problems. And guess where you have to go afterward, back to all the other problems you left at home.

In general, what people tend to neglect is to make time for reflection during those times of relaxation. Really just sitting down, quietly, thinking and analyzing oneself in relation to their goals and the disconnect that keeps them from achieving them. Are their personal issues keeping them from achieving their goals? Or is it perhaps stress at work, such as law enforcement, that is holding people back? That's why reflection is important in understanding one's setbacks.

According to Dr. Allen McConnell with PsychologyToday.com, "research in the psychological literature suggests that the negativity elicited from our awareness of a discrepancy between our current state and our goal is critical to spurring self-improvement. That is, the pain that emanates from our confronting a transgression (e.g., the person who faces a chart on his fridge that confirms his only going to the gym once in the past week) is aversive, and it is this negative feeling that motivates one to reduce the discrepancy."

Reflection also circles back to the virtue of humility and putting yourself under observation in order to keep ego in check. When you reflect to understand where your weaknesses and failures lie, you really have no choice but to humble yourself to solve the issues and come to a state of tranquility. And as Marcus Aurelius said, retreating into one's self and reflecting is the most powerful tool we have for attaining understanding and tranquility.

As for my process, I believe clearing the mind first is essential for getting myself ready for reflection. Reflection is a lot easier when the mind is clear and there are no other thoughts to distract you, so that's why I always try to do whatever activity clears my mind before I reflect.

Sometimes I like to read in the morning and then I usually begin to reflect out on my back porch with a cup of coffee, which sometimes does the trick, but most times I need to have a strenuous workout and then I lay on the floor in the middle of the squat rack with my feet up, music shut off, and I reflect.

That is where I do most of my vital problem solving of life's obstacles. I can't even begin to tell you how cathartic it is to be physically exhausted, mind completely empty, and have all these answers in your life just come to you. Much of the structure and flow of this book was conceived from those very periods of reflection.

So, make sure time is set aside, or even piggybacked onto a stress-relieving activity, to reflect and understand yourself.

Afterthoughts

"A good character is the only guarantee of long-lasting, carefree happiness."

-Seneca-
Letters from a Stoic XXVII

As I said earlier, tranquility is a sort of vigilance for your spirit. An unbroken spirit can breed good character in a person, and that, as Seneca said, is the only guarantee for life-long happiness; it boils down to achieving tranquility in your life through means of virtue and controlling your opinions and perceptions.

I wholeheartedly believe that adopting philosophy into your life is a great asset for mental health and a better alternative to substance abuse. It saved me, but may not be the answer for everyone. Sometimes seeking outside help through the means of doctors and lawfully prescribed medications is what is needed to get the healing process in full swing, but that shouldn't mean you can't have a philosophy or other holistic self-help means as a supplementation.

Doctors and medications will eventually taper off and afterward, you'll be left to your own devices; and if you have no virtue implemented in your life at that point to rely on, you may feel like you've been hung out to dry and revert back to that dark place you originated from.

Adopt a means of your choosing that will keep your spirit rock solid, your character disciplined, and your mind tranquil because that is the only guarantee of long-lasting happiness.

PART IV

DISCIPLINE

"Is it possible to be free from error? Not by any means, but it is possible to be a person always stretching to avoid error. For we must be content to at least escape a few mistakes by never letting our attention slide."

-Epictetus-
Discourses 4.12

We've reached the final virtue that is worth mentioning last, because it is the most important one. It is the one which fuels success in the other three virtues. It's the part of your psyche that whispers the voice of reason in your ear and reminds you of the hard route you should be taking instead of the easy route you want to be taking. And it's what Epictetus describes as the means to keep us from having our attention slip away from what's important in the now in order to mitigate crucial, possibly lethal, and often avoidable mistakes. This virtue is discipline.

And why is discipline so important? Because you can't utilize humility if you're not disciplined enough to tell your ego to "shut up," you can't achieve well-rounded vigilance if you're not disciplined enough to recognize your weaknesses and train yourself to be stronger, and you can't arrive at a state of tranquility if you're not disciplined enough to control your opinions and perspective in regards to obstacles in your life, and allow trivial things to eat you alive. Everything you do to be a better person and better police officer all require, to quote retired Navy Seal Officer turned author Jocko Willink, "unmitigated daily discipline."

The day you entered into the police academy, everything that you did, whether you were in tune with it or not, required a level of discipline to make sure you got through the day as physically and mentally unscathed as possible from the instructing cadre. Daily boot shining, daily uniform pressing, daily studying and preparation, daily PT, daily marching in synchronized cadence and step, daily flag raising and lowering, etc. Every day was almost identical. At first, it all seemed monotonous, or even hard and stressful to some people, but as the weeks went on, all those menial tasks became second nature and you didn't even give them a second thought, you just did them. That's how discipline works. It needs to be drilled into your mind and become a second or even primary nature to you to the point where you just do what you need to do to make yourself better without any internal push back. To quote RUC Officer Richard Latham again: "discipline in the small things breeds good habits for when it matters." He also stated how discipline creates a level of "self-control under provocation."

Seneca made a connection to ways where discipline is a natural instinct that takes no thought. In letter CXXIII, he describes to his friend Lucilius ways in which people reason with themselves, shy away from virtues and embrace vices, basically the lies we love to tell ourselves to take the easy, more pleasurable path in life, as opposed to the harder more righteous path.

He then goes on to explain how we must not fear the harder path, refrain from desiring the easy one, how we must use the nature of discipline in embracing that perspective:

> "Do you not see the difference in posture of those going downhill and those going uphill? Those who descend lean their bodies back; those who are climbing lean forward. For if you are going downhill, Lucilius, then throwing your weight forward is going along with vice, and if you are going uphill then leaning back is doing the same. It is downhill towards pleasure, but one must go uphill towards what is harsh and tough. When climbing we must drive our bodies onwards, when descending we must hold them back.

The Stoic Cop: Policing Through Stoic Virtue

Walking up a hill or mountain, much like life's goals, has its difficulties, and depending on the shape you're in, it may be very hard, but the goal is always to get to the top and see the beauty below. So, think about when we actually do physically walk uphill, we naturally shift our weight forward without even thinking about it or hesitating in order to avoid falling backward, or in the case of life's goals, failing. Much like when we walk downhill, our bodies naturally lean backward and we force ourselves to slow down to avoid falling forward, or in the case of life's pleasures, or indulging or becoming addicted.

That is how discipline should be: natural and uncompromised to ensure that we don't fail too hard in our goals, or fall too hard in our pleasures. It's all about temperance or self-regulation and staying disciplined.

The Easy Path v. The Hard Path

"Soft living imposes on us the penalty of debility."

-Seneca-
Letters from a Stoic LV

Iron ore can be made into a hard steel only after it's been forged in fire. The hardest and most precious material known to man, diamonds, can only become what they are after carbon atoms have endured millions of years of intense pressure and heat. They then have to be blasted to the surface of the earth from its mantle by means of volcanic eruption. And as police officers, or even just as human beings trying to survive the primal side of life, we too need to become hard, or as former Green Beret and UFC fighter Tim Kennedy calls it, "hard to kill." And how do you become hard to kill? Having the discipline to take the hard road.

As Seneca said, soft living debilitates us. For example, the convenience of online shopping debilitates us from going to the store and physically walking. The convenience of smartphones and GPS devices debilitates us from the knowledge of using a map or a dictionary. The convenience of online dating and hiding behind a profile debilitates us from the social skills and confidence we need to meet people whether it be romantically or not. Purposely skipping workouts, or scaling back prescribed rep ranges or weight loads debilitates us from the means to get stronger.

As police officers though, things like the convenience of a Taser debilitates us from keeping up with our defensive tactics because we become overconfident and too reliant on the tool instead of our actual skills. Career long detectives can become ignorant of the basics of officer safety in the street.

I remember one year in annual in-service training, there was a portion of defensive tactics where we had to practice handcuffing skills because that was apparently, to mention unbelievably, a recognized issue with some officers throughout the year.

Long story short, I was in class with a bunch of detectives who had been behind a desk in the criminal investigations division (CID) for years, probably decades, and who hadn't made a physical arrest in about that same length of time. Needless to say, watching them in scenario-based training attempting to remove their handcuffs from their holster, and apply them onto a simulated, mildly resistant role-player was about the saddest thing I had ever seen.

But it made me realize just how perishable a simple skill like handcuffing someone can be, and how easily sitting behind a desk for years, not being on the streets can absolutely debilitate a cop from basic functioning skills.

I am sincerely not saying that deciding to be a detective for most of your career is taking the easy way out. Detective work is absolutely an essential part in the serving of justice on behalf of victims, and some officers are really good at it, so it makes sense to do what you're good at. I mention that story as an example of how perishable simple and basic skills are if not attended to; and not forgetting to mention that in the agency I worked in at the time of the handcuffing training, people often opted to go to CID as a means to hide.

So, what defines the hard road or hard way of living? It's simple. It's surpassing the bare minimum and going above and beyond expectations. It's the road that leads you to some sort of new skill or enlightenment whether it be physically, mentally, or spiritually. It's the choice to be better because no goal worth achieving ever comes easy; it comes with failure, setbacks, and obstacles. So, remember:

"Excellence withers without an adversary."
–Seneca-

You need those failures to teach you how not to do something, you need those setbacks to keep driving you forward, and you need those obstacles to teach you how to solve problems.

The more you choose to take the hard road, the more natural taking the hard road will become and the easier it will be to overcome those obstacles and setbacks.

So, stop creating handicaps for yourself. Stop deteriorating your character by taking the easy way out of things. Taking the easy way out, and taking it often, will only lead you down that hill with a forward lean, prompting you to fall even harder.

On Staying Strict

"Be tolerant with others and strict with yourself."
-Marcus Aurelius-
Meditations

In order to maintain a strict level of discipline you have to decide to stop cutting corners, making trade-offs with yourself, rationalizing poor decisions, and following the footsteps of others who knowingly do wrong and get away with it. Just because someone else is getting away with stepping out of line does not mean you will. Expect not to get away with anything unless it's done righteously.

Too often in law enforcement, we tend to follow in the footsteps of other more tenured officers, even if it goes against policy because we see that their way is easier, they've been around longer so they should know what they're doing, and they just haven't gotten caught yet cutting those corners or being out of policy.

So, we blindly follow and do the same things instead of thinking for ourselves and doing what we know is correct. And consequently, it always seems like we're the ones who get caught and get reprimanded. Then we bring upon ourselves all this unnecessary stress that we could have avoided if we had just maintained a strict level of discipline in our work.

We need to keep in the forefront of our minds that it is we who control how to conduct ourselves in our work, not anyone else, and we shouldn't allow the less disciplined influence us. Remember:

> *"If you apply yourself to the task before you, following right reason seriously, vigorously, calmly, without allowing anything to distract but keeping your divine part pure as you might be bound to give it back immediately; if you hold to this expecting nothing, fearing nothing, but satisfied with your present activities according to nature, and with heroic truth in every word and sound which you utter, you will live happily. And there is no man who is able to prevent you from this."*
>
> –Marcus Aurelius-

Be your own master and set a standard of excellence to be achieved daily. Be better every day. Demand the best of yourself and refuse to allow anyone to influence you otherwise.

GRAB YOUR BATTLE AX AND START SWINGING

"In the morning when you rise unwillingly, let this thought be present: I am rising to the work of a human being. Why then am I dissatisfied if I am going to do the things for which I exist, and for which I was brought into the world? Or have I been made for this, to lie in the bedclothes and keep myself warm? 'But this is more pleasant!' Do you exist then to take your pleasure, and not at all for action or exertion?"

-Marcus Aurelius-
Meditations 5.1

One of my favorite motivational personalities that I follow on Instagram, who I've mentioned before, is Jocko Willink. And if you're reading this particular book, you may be a part of his audience as well. His serious and more or less stoic demeanor, with the hint of dry humor, is awesome. Always preaching methods on how to destroy the enemy who he has identified as "Monday," and keeping on "the path" thereafter. My favorite of his methods for attacking Monday was when he said to simply grab a battle ax and start swinging. He then went on to describe how people will make excuses such as not owning a battle ax, to which he seriously replies, "go down to the closest medieval armorer in your neighborhood and get one."

It's humorous but serious at the same time, and the point he is trying to make is to stop making excuses as to why things can't be done. And Marcus Aurelius had the same ideology 1500 years ago, just in a more realistic and practical manner. Basically, when waking up in the morning, you should absolutely tell yourself that there's work to be done, and should not waste that time fighting yourself and rationalizing excuses to yourself to stay in bed. It's a primitive and instinctual characteristic to have some sort of purpose. Every single living organism on this planet in some way, shape, or form has a role to play and a job to do, and they get right to it almost robotically.

But we as human beings have the gift of reasoning that almost all other living beings don't. Reasoning is what sets us apart from the rest of nature. Reasoning is what makes us civilized social creatures instead of instinctual robotic beasts, reasoning is what makes our problem-solving skills more evolved to keep technology advancing, reasoning is what makes us aware and perceptive of the world at large, but reasoning also gives us the capability, or I should say debility, to make excuses, to choose the easy path, and to become weak. And the downside of reasoning is what seems to win most often in our lives. But Seneca posed a good question in letter CXXIII as to how we can reason with ourselves to stay disciplined:

"How much better is it to pursue the right path and bring yourself to the point of where only what is honorable is satisfying to you?"

You know that the satisfaction felt from working hard, conquering obstacles, and making a difference feels a lot better than the convenience of cheating, cutting corners, and making excuses.

And yet, many cops still choose to half-ass their calls or cases because they think it may be a bunch of bullshit, they still choose to go through the motions in training, they still choose to not take ownership of the area they're riding because it's almost time to go home and they want to leave on time.

And when you choose to cut these corners, you know you feel a hint of guilt or shame (or at least you should) because you're screwing yourself or worse, someone else.

I've absolutely chosen to be weak before. I've half-assed cases that to me, were trivial, with the sole intention to get the report typed up and the case closed without having any regard for the justice that was expected to be served on behalf of the complainant. I've absolutely held out on calls (extremely rare though) at the end of a shift because it was just one of those rare occasions where I was over the crappy day and did not want to help out or stay late. To say that I've never made the conscious decision not to be disciplined would be an absolute lie.

And how did I feel afterward? Like an asshole. I would then feel the need to always make up for my lack of discipline by punishing myself. I would work extra hard the next day; taking more calls that I needed to for other officers in order to redeem myself and make it up to the others that I screwed over. Had I just been disciplined enough before to do what was expected of me as a police officer and human being, I wouldn't have had to make extra work for myself.

So, I urge you to take the harder high road and take it regularly. Do what is honorable at all times. Make it second nature to do what is right in order to free your mind of the negative feelings you get when you reason with yourself and make excuses to be weak. Doing what is honorable is always what feels satisfying.

Afterthoughts

It can never be stressed enough just how important establishing a level of discipline in your life will greatly enhance progress and achievement in all areas of your life. Like I said before, discipline is the fuel that drives success in all the other virtues, it's that important. It is just as import as actual fuel is to a vehicle.

Constantly keep your attention focused on your mission, whether it's to get promoted, get into a specialized unit, or even to get hired as a police officer if you're reading this and contemplating the profession.

Being strict with yourself will ensure that you are prepared to conquer the mission. It will prevent big mistakes that will cause big setbacks on the path. It will also show others who may be somewhat in control of your future within the agency that you care enough to be successful.

"Discipline Equals Freedom"

-Jocko Willink-

Final Thoughts

"Hold sacred your capacity for understanding. For in it is all, that our ruling principle won't allow anything to enter that is either inconsistent with nature or with the constitution of a logical creature. It's what demands due diligence, care for others, and obedience to a greater being."

-Marcus Aurelius-
Meditations 3.9

At the beginning of this book, I explained that in order to take away from this book the philosophy and wisdom expressed, you must first humble yourself and realize that your character needed improvement, as I realized it myself and now that I've detailed at length how the stoic philosophy can be applied to the common police officer, the next step is to adopt the philosophy and put it into practice.

It's not enough to simply read the quotes and aphorisms you come across and acknowledge to yourself that you agree with them and blindly regurgitate them to sound enlightened. You have to implement them in your life order to enhance your character and actually be enlightened. As Epictetus said:

> *"Those who receive the bare theories immediately want to spew them, as an upset stomach does food. First, digest your theories and you won't throw them up. Otherwise, they will be raw, spoiled and not so nourishing. After you've digested them, show us the changes is your reasoned choice, just like the shoulders of a gymnast display their diet and training, and as the craft of artisans show in what they've learned."*

On every call that you ride and every encounter you have, you should ask yourself if your reaction to whatever is unfolding is correct. Are you responding virtuously? Are you being humble or is your ego creeping up behind you? Have you prepared yourself to endure whatever is thrown at you? Are you strong enough to avoid allowing it to negatively affect you?

That is the goal of philosophy. To train yourself to have that little voice in the back of your mind constantly reminding you how to behave and react honorably; virtuously. Coming to terms with the way things are and being content with it, seeing the silver lining in everything that happens, and flipping your perspective on its head. This job does not have to eat you alive as you sometimes feel like it can. You don't have to allow yourself to be a casualty of the profession.

"There is no state of slavery more disgraceful than one which is self-imposed."

—Seneca-

In order to adopt the philosophy will probably mean a change in lifestyle. You may need to separate or distance yourself from those things that negatively affect you. And sometimes, that may mean certain people. I can say from experience sticking tight to officers who have nothing but negative things to say about your agency or the job, in general, can be very influential, especially if you're a young officer.

"If you want to get away from your vices you must get away from the examples others set for them."

—Seneca-

For me, I recognized that keeping to a night shift schedule and being in darkness and isolation all the time was my tipping point into self-destruction. So, I made it a point to sacrifice sleep in order to feel like a human again. If I got off work at 7 a.m., I forced myself to wake up by 11 a.m.

Living on less than four hours of sleep is rough, but it did the trick. It was almost like a resurgence of life was forced into my soul and it felt liberating. And from that simple alteration in my life, everything else good in my life seemed to fall right into place.

If there's anything I want to make sure that my fellow officers take away from this book, it's this: that whatever virtue you embraced from this project, you pass it on to the next person who may need it. This whole thing circles back to the very beginning and first quote I put in this book from Seneca:

> *"If wisdom were offered to me on the condition that I should keep it shut away and not divulge it to anyone, I should reject it."*

Also keep in mind that no matter how much you embrace this philosophy or any other philosophy or religion for that matter, you will still make mistakes and you will fail at times. Just make sure that when you fall, you get back up and remember the virtues instilled in you to make a comeback. Strive to have it all, but be prepared to lose even more. That is the key to persevering.

Lastly, I'll say this: that even though philosophy has changed me, I still have my moments. It is important to keep your expectations in check during your quest for betterment. The human factor will tend to take over sometimes and impulse will win. Remember:

> *"The sage—the perfect Stoic who behaves perfectly in every situation is an ideal, not an end."*

Just like all things in life, perfection is something that is unattainable. Even as you enter into the endeavor of philosophy in search for wisdom and character, you will lose your temper, you will be egotistical, you will be frustrated, and you will be lazy.

The only thing you can do is implement the daily discipline to be better than you were the day before and strive to continually be the best version of a police officer that you envision. The more you practice philosophy, the more naturally you will default to its virtues during spiritually and socially trying times. Just like the more you practice police tactics, the more naturally you'll default to them in real-life situations.

Despite my journey, there are still moments where I get angry at the slightest inconvenience, the slightest setback, the slightest rude remark I get. I am in no way a saint or a "sage." I don't know everything and never will, but stoicism has shown me how to reel myself back in, regain my composure, and continue down the path with better reasoning than I had before. I am a less stressed police officer for it, but more importantly, I am a better person for it. I have learned to control my own perceived chaos.

Bibliography

Angerer, P. D. (2017, July). Night Work and the Risk of Depression. *Deutsches Artzeblatt International, 114*. Retrieved May 20, 2020, from https://www.ncbi.nlm.nih.gov/pmc/articles/PMC5499504/

Aurelius, M. (1997). *Meditations* (Dover Thrift Edition ed.). (W. Kaufman, Ed., & G. Long, Trans.) Mineola, New York: Dover Publications. Retrieved 2018

Blue H.E.L.P. (n.d.). Retrieved April 23, 2020, from Blue H.E.L.P: https://bluehelp.org/

Browning, C. R. (1998). *Ordinary Men: Reserve Police Battalion 101 and the Final Solution in Poland.* New York: Harper Perennial.

Epictetus. (2008). *Discourses and Selected Writings* (Penguin Classics ed.). (R. Dobbin, Ed., & R. Dobbin, Trans.) London, England: Penguin Group. Retrieved 2019

Gill, C. (2015, November 21). *What is Stoic Virtue?* Retrieved 2019, from https://modernstoicism.com: https://modernstoicism.com/what-is-stoic-virtue-by-chris-gill/

Gilmartin, K. M. (2002). *Emotional Survival for Law Enforcement: A Guide for Officers and their Families.* E-S Press.

Holiday, R. (2016). *Ego is the Enemy.* New York, New York, USA: Penguin Group. Retrieved 2019

Holiday, R., & Hanselman, S. (2016). *The Daily Stoic.* (S. Hanselman, Trans.) New York, New York, USA: Penguin Random House LLC.

Latham, R. (2001). *Deadly Beat: Inside the Royal Ulster Constabulary.* Edinburgh: Mainstream Publishing Company.

Machiavelli, N. (1999). *The Prince.* Signet Classics.

McConnell, A. R. (2010, September 18). *Reflection critical for self-improvement.* Retrieved from Psychology Today: https://www.psychologytoday.com/us/blog/the-social-self/201009/reflection-critical-self-improvement

Peterson, S. (2018, June 6). Parkland Officer Scot Peterson: 'This Will Haunt Me The Rest Of My Life'. (S. Guthrie, Interviewer) YouTube. Retrieved from https://www.youtube.com/watch?v=1jVZOl4x3L8

Seneca. (2004). *Letters from a Stoic.* (B. Radice, Ed., & R. Campbell, Trans.) London, England: Penguin Group.

Silver, J. (Producer), Henry, D. L., Henkin, H. (Writers), & Herrington, R. (Director). (1989). *Road House* [Motion Picture]. MGM.

Stockdale, J. B. (1993). *Courage Under Fire: Testing Epictetus' Doctrines in a Laboratory of Human Behavior.* Stanford, California: Hoover Essays. Retrieved 2019

Stofan, J. (2019, June 18). *Former Broward County Sheriff Scott Israel makes case for reinstatement.* Retrieved from WJHG: https://www.wjhg.com/content/news/Former-Sheriff-Scott-Israel-makes-case-for-reinstatement-511484302.html

Sun-tzu. (1994). *The Art of War.* (R. D. Sawyer, Trans.) New York, New York, USA: Fall River Press.

Szoldra, P. (2018, September 26). *Mattis: This is the one Book Everyone Should Read.* Retrieved March 24, 2020, from Task & Purpose: https://taskandpurpose.com/code-red-news/mattis-favorite-book

Umhau, J. C. (2013, January 4). Low Vitamin D Status and Suicide: A Case-Control Study of Active Duty Military Service Members. (K. Hashimoto, Ed.) *PloS One.* doi:https://www.ncbi.nlm.nih.gov/pmc/articles/PMC3537724/

Villers, P. (2016, February 27). *The Police Officer as a Stoic.* Retrieved from Modern Stoicism: https://modernstoicism.com/the-police-officer-as-stoic-by-peter-villiers/

Willink, J. (2017). *Discipline Equals Freedom Field Manual.* St. Martin's Press.

Willink, J., Berke, D., & Armstrong, S. (2020). *The Code. The Evaluation. The Protocols: Striving to Become an Eminently Qualified Human Being.* Jocko Publishing.

Wolfe, D. (2017, November 8). *5 tips from Force Science on de-escalation tactics.* Retrieved from Police One: https://www.policeone.com/crisis-intervention-training/articles/5-tips-from-force-science-on-de-escalation-tactics-cftKqoOW-GC7SGopa/

Xenophon. (2014). *Memorabilia.* Ithica, New York: Cornell University Press.

www.ingramcontent.com/pod-product-compliance
Lightning Source LLC
Chambersburg PA
CBHW070042040426
42333CB00041B/2070